MW01231914

FROM BABYLON TO RASTAFARI:
ORIGIN AND HISTORY OF THE RASTAFARIAN MOVEMENT

by DOUGLAS R. A. MACK

**Published by Research Associates
School Times Publications
Frontline Distribution Int'l Inc.
Chicago. Jamaica. London. Republic of
Trinidad and Tobago.**

Printed in the United States of America

First Printing 1999

06 05 04 03 02 01   5 4 3 2

Cover Design by Denise Borel

Library of Congress Cataloging-in-Publication Data
98-66863

Mack, Douglas,
          From babylon to rastafari: origin and his-
tory of the rastafarian movement/ Douglas Mack.
          p. cm.

ISBN:0-94839-047-6

FROM BABYLON TO RASTAFARI:
ORIGIN AND HISTORY OF THE RASTAFARIAN MOVEMENT

"Ethiopia had many problems to attend to. However, it would welcome the Rastafarian brethren to reside here. "

Emperor Haile Sellassie I, April, 1965 Addis Ababa (Address to the second Rastafarian mission to Africa).

By DOUGLAS R. A. MACK

Foreword by DOUGLAS R. EWART,
Adjunct Professor, Art Institute of Chicago.
Edited and Introduction By:
RAS SEKOU SANKARA TAFARI

This book is dedicated to the memory of all the Rastafarian pioneering patriots; those who have left us and those who are still with us; whose unselfish lives on the camps fostered the brotherhood of the Rastafarian culture.

"A Nation without the knowledge of its past history is like a tree without its roots."

Marcus M. Garvey

His foundation is in the holy mountains.
The Lord loveth the gates of Zion more than all the dwellings of Jacob.
Glorious things are spoken of thee, O city of Jah. Se'lah.
I will make mention of Rahab and Babylon to them that know I: behold Philistia, and Tyre, with Ethiopia; this man was born there.
And of Zion it shall be said, This and that man was born in her: and the highest himself shall establish her.
The Lord shall count, when he writeth up the people, that this man was born there. Se'lah.
As well the singers as the players on instruments shall be there: all my springs are in thee.

Psalm 87

Contents

FOREWORD

I was most honored and elated when Douglas Mack asked me to compose a statement regarding the book *Origin and History of The Rastafarian Movement*. I have known Douglas Mack from my early childhood. I was born and reared at 5 Sheffield Road in Eastern Kingston. Duggie, or Brother Duggie, as we affectionately call him, lived across the street with his parents and several generations of his family. His grandfather, Pappy Aiken was a potter of great renown, who ran a successful earthenware factory immediately across the street from my grandmother, Florence Fowler-Kelly's house. I remember several occasions on which my father, Thomas Ewart, would ask Duggie to bring me to Wembley Cricket Club to meet him there during my father's umpiring of cricket matches. I remember those times with great relish, Duggie's company was most gratifying. He was a very mentally and spiritually mature young adult who was always assuring and encouraging.

As the other youngsters and I in the area grew up, Brother Duggie was to become a beacon/mentor for all of us. Duggie was always a positive and convivial spirit! Many of my schoolmates and I spent countless Fridays after school at Brother Duggie's house on Windward Road and Sheffield Road, in groundation, discussing every imaginable subject. Brother Duggie's house was a gathering place for people from all walks of life and for Rastafarians in particular. I would, on occasion, run into my most beloved cousin, Herman (Woody) King, a member of the Rastafarian Movement, as well as scores of kindred spirits that I would become increasingly familiar with in ensuing years at Duggie's house. Brother Duggie always emphasized the importance of getting a good formal and street education. Duggie would always say,

> "Rasta people must be well educated in order to free Africa yu know. Yu kant go back to Africa without an education, without a skill."

The area in which we grew up was an area of cultural, intellectual, spiritual, and social ferment. There were many people in our vicinity who were Garveyites, my grandmother was one, and I remember policeman Case, who lived just a few doors from us, was also a strong Garveyite. We were all acutely aware of the positive nature of Africa, as a result of being in the midst of these cognizant people. Mr. Case was one of the most positive law enforcement agents I have ever known. He would come over to Donchaster: The Boy Scout's Headquarters in Jamaica at that time and discuss Garveyism with every imaginable soul. As the years passed, Douglas Mack would become a pivotal figure in the Rastafarian Movement. He was a member of both "Back to Africa Delegations." The delegation was entrusted with the responsibility of procuring sanctions from various African governments that would facilitate Repatriation from Jamaica to Africa.

We so often read books which are written by people who have only a cursory knowledge of intricate subject of the Rastafarian Movement. It is indeed a blessing and a major milestone to have this book, a most in-depth and crucial chronicle penned by Douglas Mack, a man who has been inextricably connected to the Rastafarian Movement, from his youth to his sage maturity.

Douglas R. Ewart
composer, musician, visual artist and craftsperson
adjunct professor, School of the Art Institute of Chicago

Introduction

"If there is no struggle, there is no progress; and there is no progress without struggle." Frederick Douglass

The *Origin and History of the Rastafarian Movement* is a splendid piece of work, written on a remarkable, dynamic and indigenous movement such as the Rastafarians by one of it's ardent followers.The first chapter entitled 'Histrionics' is very potent. The author, Ras Douglas Mack, acting as both a griot and historian delves into the 'Kebra Nagast': the Glory of Kings. He unfolds the incient love story between King Solomon of Jahrasalem and the Empress Makeda of Sheba a large province in Ethiopia. He tells the story as only an iriginal Rastafarian elder can present it, that is with much candor and wittiness.

This commences the historic lineage from King Solomon, the son of King David, to the Emperor Haile Sellassie I, the 225th and final Emperor so far to have sat on King David's throne.

In Chapter II, 'The Heritage' Brother Duggie speaks about the role of the Falashas or 'Ethiopia Jewry' and their continuation and upkeep of the Solomonic dynastay up to this time of the I Majesty-Emperor Haile Sellassie I, also known as Ras Tafari. However, in Chapter III, 'Jamaica—It's Ethos' the writer reveals the early history of the island originally called Xyamaca (Jamaica): "the land of wood and water."

Xyamaca was the name the Arawak Indians who were the island's early inhabitants called it. He outlines Columbus' voyage when he accidentally stumbled on the

island in 1494, and seized it from the natives in the name
of King Ferdinand and Queen Isabella of Spain. Later on,
the Spanish colonist began their trek to Jah-ma-kya where
they colonized and enslaved the native peoples. In this
chapter he mentions how Queen Elizabeth I, commissioned her cousin, John Hawkins with a fleet of ships so
as to increase the slave trade between the ports of Africa
and what was then called the British West Indies. Sir
Hawkins, as he was later called, (after he was knighted)
for his role in seizing large groups of Africans from off the
coast of Africa. He turned them into human cargo on his
fleet of slavers, of which his flagship was named the S.S.
Jesus of Lubeck. The chapter refers to Sir Henry Morgan,
a notorious Pirate who was appointed the first British
Governor of the island. It deals also with the emancipation of the African slaves in 1834-1838, and the coming of
the East Indians to Jah-ma-kya. Of uttermost importance
in this chapter is the 'Garvey Era.' The writer links the
Garvey   period   with   Jamaica   modern   politricks.
Therefore, the Marcus Garvey movement was not only
the forerunner to the Rastafarian movement but acted as
a catalyst for the modern day nation politricks in Jamaica,
other Caribbean islands and Africa. It was Garvey, by
way of the U.N.I.A. who inspired the forming of the West
Indian Federation, and eventually the achievement of so-
called political independence within the Caribbean and
Africa. In other words, Garvey helped to dismantle the
mental chains of colonialism, which ushered into existence neo-colonialism.

The writings in this book are very concrete and
vivid. Although I cannot literally vouch the accuracy of
some dates and events mentioned here. (In Chapter Four
he speaks of the supposedly held meeting of the Prince
Regent Ras Tafari with other African patriots, including

Marcus Garvey to form the secret order of the Nyabinghi). However, the reasonings are very sincere and sound, and it definitely comes out of the Iriginal Rastafarian Jahrasalem School of Thought.

In Chapter Four, 'Rastafari the Dawn,' he writes that:

> "Thus the Honorable Marcus Garvey sets the stage to herald in the era of His Imperial Majesty, the Emperor Haile Sellassie I, Conquering Lion of the Tribe of Judah."

He indicates that there was a political void in Jamaica after Garvey left to set up his office in London, England. Jamaica and other parts of the Caribbean were strive torn, there were mass social, labor and political unrest in Jamaica (and Trinidad and Tobago) during the 1930's. Hence, the Rastafarian movement began to be more noticeable, and this ignited a new spirit of resistance among the downpressed masses of people, especially after the coronation of the Negus Negusti, the King of all Kings, Haile Sellassie I on November 2nd 1930: and the commencement of the war between Italy and Ethiopia in 1935.

In Chapter Five, 'Concepts of the Rastafarian' Brother Mack gets straight to the point, when he writes: "All Rastafarian brethren hold sacred three basic concepts of the culture."

1) That H.I.M. Emperor Haile Sellassie of Ethiopia is the returned Messiah, the Godhead, the Ancient of the Days.
2) That all the African peoples brought to the Western hemisphere through the advent of European

slave trading, whose progeny still survives, have the
inherent rights to demand their repatriation back to the
African continent if so desired.
    3) That Ethiopia is an integral part of the Garden of
Eden, as recorded in the book of Genesis"

    This chapter provides both "biblical and historical
concordance" to the Rastafarian way of life, conception
and history. Brother Mack gives an actual outline of the
early Rastafarian gatherings in Chapter Six: "The
Camps." The griot refers to the democratization within
the Rastafarian movement. It was at the camps that decisions were made and the Bible, the Holy Piby, the
Promised Key, and other historical books, social events,
i.e. past and current activities were discussed and
resolved using ultimate democratic procedures.   The
early Rastafarians were well schooled on current events
as the Ethiopian War of 1935-1941. Brother Duggie also
mentions the gatherings at Pinnacle Hill, and the first
Rastafarian community to be assembled there, under the
auspices of its founder and first recorded Rastafarian to
date—Brother Leonard Percival Howell. In this chapter,
one gets a brief insight as to how Pinnacle was estab -
lished and governed; and how the economic ventures
were based on naturalism and living off the land.
    Pinnacle was built on self-reliance and interdepen-
dence. The cultivation of Ganja, marijuana, was well
known. Cannabis Sativae was the main cash crop. In
addition to agriculture, there were Rastafarian craft and
artisan people, i.e. skilled brothers and dawtas, who were
trained as carpenters, masons, plumbers, shoemakers,
machinists, tailors, seamstresses, etc, all of whom con -
tributed to the upkeep of the Pinnacle community.

> "A council of elders was established to assist in
> the daily administration of the camp, and to
> maintain discipline among the brethren who
> dwelt there." The camp at Pinnacle expanded
> to embrace hundreds of brethren, some who
> resided and some who were frequent visitors."

The writer/historian acting as griot relates some
juicy gossip on the camp about Brother Howell on his
release from prison, and his return to Pinnacle. However,
in this editor's mind, this story should not be of much significance to the reader, especially since it's based on
hearsay or circumstantial information, and even though it
might be proven to be true at a later date, this should not
negate or blemish the momentous works ascribed to
Brother Leonard Percival Howell, for being the architect
of the first ever Rastafarian community.

The most important message in this book, *From
Babylon to Rastafari: Origin and History of the Rastafarian
Movement*, is delivered in this chapter on the camps, when
the elder, Brother Mack unfolds the one true and binding
tenet of the Rastafari concept —the Ivinity of Emperor
Haile Sellassie I, thus making H.I.M. the omnipotent, the
omniscient, the living Irator, the king of all kings, the
Power of the Hola Trinity. In this candid document, he
acknowledges Brother Leonard Howell as the first recorded Rastafarian.

> "Brother Leonard Percival Howell was the first
> recorded Rastafarian brethren who openly
> preached the divinity of H.I.M. Emperor Haile
> Sellassie I, as the returned messiah, the
> Godhead in flesh."

The author tells us about the numerous camps outside and around the Kingston and Spanish Town districts, including Prince Emmanuel Charles Edwards of the Ackee Walk camp in Spanish Town.

> "The police constantly harassed these brethren. Eventually there was an inflagration in 1960 during a Rastafarian convention at Prince Emmanuel's camp. Over ninety Rastafarian brethren were arrested, including Prince Emmanuel."

Soon after the disturbances, the Prince moved his camp farther away from Spanish Town, and eventually he settled in Bull Bay, high up on the hills surrounding what some referred to as "the bloody shitty" of Kingston. Prince Emmanuel's camp is now a formidable house within the Rastafarian mansion. They are now referred to as "Bobo Shanty." They are still assembled at Bull Bay, although Prince Emmanuel departed the flesh sometime in May 1993. Brother Mack paints a picture of blissfulness when he outlines:

> "The camps were the places of retreat from Babylonian pressures of life, where we acquired our spiritual meditation. We became avid scholars of the Bible, reading, reasoning, and interpreting the passages while chanting our songs of praises to the "Most High." The spirit of the camp created a soothing balm to the aching soul."

The author allocated a section for the Rastafarian sistren who were active on the camps in the early days. Brother Duggie, in writing about the sistren, has lauded them majestically. He gives the dawtas total respect and reverence. He refers to the Rastawomen as "the daughters of Zion" and writes passionately on their involve - ment and their activities.

> "The sisters were a tower of strength in the daily activities on the camp."

The book indicates how the dawtas of Zion would participate in the struggles for our way of life, and the tactics they embarked on to ensure Rasta survived. It speaks of their natural beauty, their execution of finesse and charm when dealing with the police, etc. in other words, the Rastafarian woman was and is the forward bone—the mother of the Rastafarian movement.

The Honorable Marcus Garvey's profound description of the African woman fits the Rastafarian woman of that period adequately, when he said:

> "What the night is to the day, is woman to man. The period of change that brings us light out of darkness, darkness out of light, and semi-light out of darkness are like the changes we find in woman day to day. She makes one happy, then miserable.   You are kind, then unkind. Constant yet unconstant.   Thus we have woman. No real man can do without her."

However, the author/historian did not mention in this chapter or anywhere else in the book, about the growing concept of the dreadlocks. He has not mentioned when it was first adapted as part of the Rastafarian way of life; or when it was first introduced into Jamaica, and by whom. He did not write or recall the growing contra-

dictions on the camps between combheads or the beardman Rastafarians, and those brethren and sistren who
accepted the Nazarite way of adorning their heads with
the crown of thorns—in the form of dreadlocks. Indeed,
there would have been contradictions on the camps, as
well as on the first ifficial mission to Africa in 1961,
between these two factions of Rastafarians. In addition,
Brother Duggie fails to refer to Joseph Nathaniel Hibbert,
Archibald Dunkley or Robert Hinds as some of the early
apostles of the Rastafarian movement.

The coming together of the brethren and sistren in
inison, chanting and singing, giving Isis to the Emperor
Haile Sellassie I for the day, sometimes a week or so, celebrating a special event, for example the coronation of the
I Majesty or His earthday on July 23rd will be a reason to
have a Groundation.   Chapter Six is entitled
"Groundation." and Brother Mack defines it vividly,
when he writes:

"A Groundation was an all day, all night celebration, when brethren and sistren would
assemble at a particular camp for a special occasion...Groundation included the recital of
prayers, poems, chanting of songs and biblical
passages. The beating of the Akete (drums) was
an integral part of the Rastafarian chanting."

A Groundation also dealt with reasonings on important topics of current interest to the faithful. The griot
points out that at the Groundations.

"There were open debates which were often
highly opinionated, ardent, furious and emotional during prolong sessions. These sessions

sometimes last for days, yet without personal animosity toward any individual speaker."

Chapter Eight, "My Rastafarian Journey" the author Douglas R.A. Mack in the role as griot, recalls his first encounter with the early Rastafarians in Kingston, Jamaica, in the forties and fifties.

"At about age twelve (mid-1940's) I went on a journey with my cousin Zorro to Brother lover's camp in Warieka Hills. It was here that I met Brother lover for the first time. With his full bearded features, he had a strong resemblance to the Emperor Haile Sellassie... I was in awe, until he greeted me with a warm, "Love youth man!" I was dumbfounded. I sat with my cousin and listened to the chanted Psalms, some of which I already knew, and I became more at ease."

He continues,

"...From my experience between Count Ossie's and Brother lover's camps, I realized that the Rastafarians were a peaceful and religious group of people. I began to reason more with many of them in my neighborhood as I became older."

Nonetheless, by the early to mid-fifties, it seems that Brother Douglas was already steeped in the doctrine of Rastafari, and had become a staunch Rastafarian engulfed in the principles of the movement. Thus, by 1959, after being unjustly fired from his job with the

Alumina Jamaica Bauxite Plant, he writes:

"...so i returned home to Windward Road
where the local youngsters assembled around
me."

He established his own camp, and became a fully-
fledged organizer for the Rastafarian movement. The
early Rastafarians were distinguished by their beards.
Douglas Mack, as a young brethren testifies about the discriminatory practices of the Jamaican ruling class towards
the bearded Rastaman and he documents the violence
meted out to the brethren by the colonial police force. The
1960 Babylon savage attack on the Rastafarians gathered
at the convention called by Prince Emmanuel Charles
Edwards propelled some young academics   from the
University of the West Indies at Mona Campus, to com-
mence an independent investigation into the Rastafarian
movement.

"In 1960, an investigative report on the
Rastafarian movement was compiled by a team
of social scientists from the University of the
West Indies. This team consisted of Professor
M.J. Smith, Professor Roy Angier, and Rex
Nettleford."

After conducting lengthy interviews and research,
the scholars compiled an extensive report that revealed:

"The Rastafarian brethren had genuine complaints which required the attention of the government. The report stated that the Rastafarian
brethren should not be discriminated against in

their endeavor to obtain employment, that there should be no discrimination against Rastafarians growing their beard, that the police should not take punitive action against them for assembling on the camps, and that the Jamaican government should contact African governments, particularly Ethiopia, on the brethren's desire to repatriate back to Africa."

It was out of these detailed recommendations, that Premier Norman Manley accepted in principle, and therefore contacted a number of African governments about the idea of repatriating the Rastafarians. Five African governments responded to the call. They were Ethiopia, Ghana, Nigeria, Liberia and Sierre Leone. Following these recommendations, the first ifficial government mission to Africa manifested in April 1961.

"The team selected for the mission was comprised of Brother Philmore Alvaranga, Brother Mortimo Planno and I (Brother Douglas Mack), as representatives of the Rastafarian brethren. Other members of the mission included Mr. Westmore Blackmore of the Universal Negro Improvement Association (U.N.I.A.), Dr. M.B. Douglas of the Afro. Caribbean Council, Mr. Z. Monroe-Scarlett of the Afro-West Indian Welfare League, Mr. Cecil G. Gordon of the Ethiopian World Federation Inc., Dr. L.C. Leslie as leader and advisor of the mission and Mr. Victor Reid as the journalist. The Jamaican delegation was later joined by the Honourable E.H. Lake who was the minister of social welfare in

Antigua."

The three (3) wise brethren met with the I Majesty,
Haile Sellassie I, Osagefo, Dr. Kwame Nkrumah of Ghana
and the other leaders of the African states that they visited. The overall response regarding repatriation was very
positive.

Soon after returning to Jamaica, the Rastafarian
members of the mission compiled a report and summary
of the tour and submitted it to the Jamaica Parliament for
their deliberations. This report was signed by Philmore
Alvaranga, Mortimo Planno, and Douglas Mack. The
other delegates compiled a separate report for the government without any input from the Rastafarian brethren.

However, Brother Mack concludes this chapter by
reporting about the vicious attack carried out by the colonial Jamaican police force "led by detective Ted Ansel" on
his camp in Warieka Hills. Nonetheless, the Rastafarian
struggle continues.

After the breakdown of the West Indian Federation,
the new Jamaican government, headed by Premier
William Alexander Bustamante did not give much support to continue the dialogue between the five African
nations visited, and his newly formed government so as
to embark on the repatriation process.

In fact, immediately after the Coral Gardens unrest
of 1963, the relationship between the police and the
Rastafarians became very antagonistic. Many
Rastafarians were beaten, maimed, killed or jailed, following the Coral Gardens civil disturbances. (Babylon
alleged that there was a Rastafarian attack on the Coral
Gardens Gas station on Hola Thursday, April 11th, 1963.
There were eight fatal casualties. Three Rastafarians, two
police officers and three tourists were killed. Two

Rastafarians described as cultists by the Daily Gleaner were arrested on murder charges. Coral Gardens is an area situated near Montego Bay).

It was out of the frustration and negative attitudes of the Bustamante regime, that the second mission to Africa was born in 1963. Little support was received from the Jamaican government and from some of the African countries visited, especially Nigeria. The other countries visited were Kenya and Ethiopia.

This book must not be taken lightly, more so, by the young Rastafarian faithfuls. It depicts some of the struggles of the early patriots on and off the camps. it demonstrates the unprovoked brutality carried out by the Babylonian shitstem towards the Rastafarian community from it's inception, when most of the idren did not wear dreadlocks, but grew beards. The victimization and discriminatory practices imposed by the colonial and later neo-colonial society are all documented within the confines of these pages.

Though the book *From Babylon to Rastafari: Origins and history of the Rastafarian Movement* is not a thorough script on the subject; example, valuable data for this editor would be the reports that the three (3) brethren signed and gave to the Jamaican Parliament from both the 1961 and 1963 repatriation missions to Africa. Also, there could have been more matter provided about Pinnacle Hill. As a matter of fact, it seems that the writings here are very autobiographical. However, the book gives the reader enough insight and food for thought, that InI can be evermindful of the struggles and persecution experienced by the elder brethrens and sistrens who sacrificed immensly (some paid dearly with their lives) so all the modern day Rasta pickneys might live.

InI must never forget upon whose backs InI now climb upon in this Rastafari trod to reach Mount Zion. InI

should always remember the patriots such as Brother
Leonard Howell, Brother Joseph Nathaniel Hibbert, Ras
Boanerges, Sam Brown, Count Ossie, Ras Mortimo
Planno, Prince Emmanuel, and a host of other legendary
elders (idrens and sistrens) who struggled relentlessly for
the Rastafarian cause.

Brother Douglas Mack must be commended for this
crafty contribution which must be added to the writ of the
Rastafarian archives. History will remember his pioneering role, as one of the three (3) Rastafarian emissaries,
who were part of the Jamaican government sponsored
ifficial mission to Africa in 1961, seeking repatriation. He
returned to Africa in 1963 to 1965, as a member of an independent repatriation mission following up on the
ground-work laid by the 1961 mission.

His meetings with the I Majesty, both on African and
Jamaican soils, are indeed a blessing, and are memorable
events that one should hold very sacred. The works and
writings herein must be examined, not the man, i.e.
whether the idren has locks, or has ever worn locks is not
a crucial issue at this moment. The contribution to the
written word, and his effort to the Rastafarian cause is of
great value.

Therefore, this book should be used as a school text
for students studying about the Rastafarian movement.
InI must salute this piece of work. It is a must read, for all
who are interested in any early documented history of a
glorious, magnificent and phenomenal movement from
one who was baptized in it's scorching fire.

Ras Sekou Sankara Tafari
Sellassie I, Pefect Love always.
January '99

RASTAFARI WORDOLOGY
Glossary of words used in Introduction

1. Babylon—Colonial/neo-colonial society, police
2. Baldhead/Combhead Rastafarian—a Rastafarian who does not grow dreadlocks but has natural hair.
3. Beardman—a Rastafarian who has grown a beard, but whose head is not matted with locks.
4. Brethren—brothers
5. Dawtas—Daughters/woman folk
6. Downpressed—oppressed
7. Dreadlocks—matted hair, grown naturally from the roots of the scalp without combing plaiting the hair.
8. Earthday—birthday
9. Hola—Holy
10. Idren—Brother
11. Ifficial—Official
12. IMajesty—His Majesty
13. Incient—Ancient
14. InI—Us, we
15. Inison—Unison
16. Irator—Creator
17. Ises—Praises
18. Ivinity—Divinity
19. Jah-mah-kya—Jamaica
20. Pickneys—Rasta children
22. Politricks—Politics
23. Sistren—Sister(s)
24. Shitstem—System
25. Shitty—City

Chapter One
HISTRIONICS

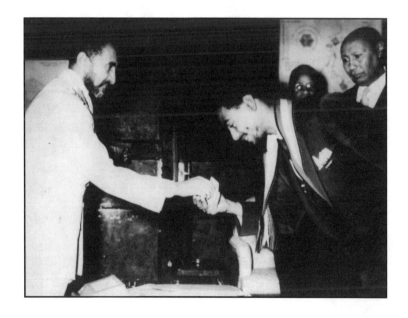

Brother Douglas Mack, receiving medal of honor from
H.I. Majesty Emperor Haile Sellassie I during Jamaica's
Back to Africa Delegation. Addis Ababa. April 1961.

HISTRIONICS

Recorded in the book "The Kebra Nagast" (The Glory of Kings) and the Holy Bible, 1st Book of Kings, Chapter 10, 2nd Chronicles, Chapter 9 is the meeting of King Solomon of Jerusalem and the Empress Baulkis Makeda known as the Queen of Sheba.

The Legend goes that King Solomon summoned the princes and rulers, of his kingdom and surrounding realms, to witness his wisdom and greatness. Solomon communicated with the birds and beasts to be present at particular times. King Solomon noted the absence of a particular bird called the "Hopi", so the king sent out other birds to search for the Hopi and bring it back so that it could be chastised for its tardiness.

After a while, the Hopi appeared before Solomon, and the king demanded an explanation for his tardiness. The Hopi explained that his lateness was not by design, but by time, distance, and sights over an area (bordered on the great waters by the Red Sea) he had never before explored.

The bird said, "My lord, I flew over a very fabulous land, full of exotic flowers, flowing streams, verdant pastures, and beautiful people, ruled by a woman-a queen. The people knew how to read and write. The men did not know how to fight or make war, but are highly skilled. They wore garland of flowers, and sang and danced happily."

King Solomon demanded to know why he was not informed of this before, and he wanted to know where this land was. The other birds replied that they had never

seen this place and only the Hopi could supply him with
the information he needed. The Hopi told them that he
had only visited the place once. King Solomon then gave
the Hopi a letter to deliver to the Queen, inviting her to
visit the Court of Solomon.

The Hopi then flew to the land he had recently discovered and delivered the note to the queen. The Queen
of Sheba and her people were delighted at the invitation
of such an illustrious king. They had heard of the existence of such a kingdom before and about the king's wisdom. (1st Kings, chapter3:v 16-28).The queen gave the
Hopi a reply, accepting King Solomon's invitation to visit
him in Jerusalem at a certain time.

King Solomon then sent out his emissaries to guar-
antee the queen's safe passage through Gaza, and into
Jerusalem. The Hopi was sent back to the queen with the
guarantee of her entourage's safe passage for the journey.
The land seen by the Hopi was Ethiopia ruled by the
Queen of Sheba, Empress Baulkis Makeda.

The Queen of Sheba then journeyed to Jerusalem,
with her royal entourage to visit King Solomon, King of
Israel. Having heard of Solomon's fame and wisdom, the
Queen set out to prove for herself, the wisdom of this
great King of Israel. (The Bible, 11, Chronicles, Chapter 9,
"The Kebra Nagast", The Glory of Kings). e.g.   The
Empress brought a great train of camels with many gifts
for Solomon, including herbs, spices, perfumes, gold, and
diamonds from Ethiopia. The   queen came to prove
Solomon with hard questions. The queen set up two bou-
quets of flowers, one was real and the other artificial but
exquisitely made.   Both were exact in resemblance.
Solomon was asked to select the real flowers without
touching them.   So identical, were the flowers that the
king was puzzled. He sent for some bees from his hive;

they pitched on the real flowers while ignoring the artificial ones. The queen was amazed at his thoughtful solution, so she decided to try his wisdom with a puzzle. "There were seven that issues, nine that enters, two that brews the draught, and one that drinks it." After pondering awhile, King Solomon replied, "Seven are the days of a woman's defilement, nine the months of pregnancy, two are the breast that brews the draught, and one the child that drinks it." Empress Makeda was amazed at King Solomon's wisdom, and replied, "Truly thou art wise."

King Solomon prepared a feast to fete the queen and her entourage. The dishes were of variety and specially prepared with many spices, of all designs. After the feasting, King Solomon and the Queen of Sheba made a pact, which was to never take anything from each other by force, only by mutual consent. It was agreed upon by both parties. That night the king and queen slept in separate royal chambers partitioned only by finely woven curtains. However, Solomon had placed an earthenware jar of water by his bedside. During the night, the spicy foods eaten by the queen increased her thirst immensely. She had to have a drink of water, but curiously there was none in her chamber. Unable to contain her thirst, the Empress proceeded to intrude into the king's chamber to secure a drink. As she lifted the cup to her head to drink, King Solomon arose, clasped his hand on hers and said, "Now you have broken your vow, release me of mine." Solomon's wisdom was again proven. The rest is history.

Queen Makeda of Sheba bore Solomon a son, Menelik. He later became Emperor Menelik I of Ethiopia. King Solomon had many wives and many sons, among them Jeroboham, Rheoboam, Absalom, and Menelik. The "Kebra Nagast" further records that the Queen of Sheba's visit to Jerusalem lasted a few months, during which time she became aware of her pregnancy with Solomon's offspring, but she had to return to her realms. So King Solomon prepared her camel train with many precious gifts. He had made a special ring with his royal seal, which was cut in two halves. One half he kept and the other was given to the Queen of Sheba to be given to his child on his twelfth birthday. Then the child was to be sent back from Ethiopia to his royal court in Jerusalem, for his upbringing and tutoring in the prerogatives of the Royal Realms. So the Queen of Sheba journeyed back to Ethiopia and bore her son.

At the age of twelve Menelik was sent back to Jerusalem with his half of the ring bearing Solomon's Royal Seal and escorted by some Ethiopian tutors. Young Menelik grew up in Solomon's Royal Court and acquired much knowledge and some of his illustrious father's wisdom.

Chapter Two
THE HERITAGE

When King Solomon became old and stricken with age, the sages, tutors, and ministers of his royal cabinet decided that a successor to the kingdom must be selected without delay. This anxiety was caused because Prince Absalom died, having been hung by his hair. Jeroboham and the other princes were at war with each other about dividing the assets of the kingdom among themselves.

Only Prince Menelik remained faithful to his father and his kingdom. So the ministers of the court decided that the time had come to make a judgment. They prepared replicas of the artifacts of the kingdom. A copy of each of the following articles was prepared: the Royal Golden Throne of David, the Ark of the Covenant, the Golden Orb, the Golden Sceptre, the royal seal of David, and the royal crown of David. (The Kebra Nagast). These artifacts along with books and other articles were secretly and meticulously copied. Meanwhile, Prince Menelik was being prepared by the ministers to return to Ethiopia.

During this time the realms of Solomon was disintegrating with various fractions at war with each other. Jeroboham was terrorizing the kingdom; so was Rheoboham. Finally, the sages made their decision. The original artifacts of the realms were all given to Prince Menelik, together with a large cabinet of ministers, religious teachers, and sages. Special instructions were constituted to preserve the heritage of King David and King Solomon, and the continuance of the Solomonic Dynasty by progeny. Prince Menelik journeyed back to Ethiopia

with his entourage, the Royal Golden Throne of David,
the Royal Crown of David, the Golden Orb of David, the
Golden Sceptre, and the religious academic and cultural
teachings of the court of Solomon. He also took with him
the Ark of the Covenant.

His arrival in Ethiopia was greeted with great adula-
tion. Empress Baulkis Makeda (Queen of Sheba and
Seba), resigned as overlord and queen of the realms.
Prince Menelik was crowned in Ethiopia as the Emperor
Menelik I, King of the Ethiopian realms. Thus began the
fabled history of Ethiopian Jewry "The Falhasha's", and
the continuance of the Solomonic Dynasty perpetuated in
Ethiopia throughout the ages to Emperor Menelik II, and
most recently His Imperial Majesty the Emperor Haile
Sellassie I.

It is important to note the continuance of Ethiopia as
a country throughout the millennium of time and ages,
from the earliest of recorded history, and through the very
reference in the first book of the bible   "Genesis".
Ethiopia stood strong despite continued Caucasian intru-
sion and invasion. It remained rooted through repeated
invasion attempts by hordes of Muslim fanatics and
attacks by the Italian armies of General Grazziano in
1896, whose forces were defeated at the Battle of Adowa
by Emperor Menelik II.

The fascist Italian savage invasion of 1935, ordered
by the Italian dictator Benito Mussolini was routed and
crushed in 1941 by patriotic Ethiopian forces, led by His
Imperial Majesty Emperor Haile Sellassie I, king of kings,
with General Ras Kassa, and the English forces led by
General Wingate. Ethiopia has truly taken its place in history as a remarkable country with a rich culture.

It must be noted at this juncture of heritage that the
man named Jesus Bar Joseph, called Jesus Christ, was

born through this Solomonic lineage; no mystery but simply progeny continuance. This man, though born of the royal lineage of David, could not claim a throne because of the disintegration of the Solomonic kingdom. Thus, there were constant invasions of middle eastern countries by Euro-Levanties and Caucasian hordes, seeking food and shelter from Europe's harsh winters. Furthermore, the population of these middle eastern countries were over-run by the hordes of Euro Caucasians who now dominate the area to this day. Therefore, Jesus Bar Joseph was a stranger in his own house from birth. He was profiled with a pigment of burnt brass and woolly hair, the Africa's class. Europe's artist missed their mark and made the portrait of Christ look not dark, but of Caucasian features. Matthew, Chapter 1, proves that Jesus

Christ was indeed defacto Joseph's son because Joseph was the exiled king of Israel indeed, by blood lineage. Therefore Jesus was by flesh, the true king of Israel in exile. Since that blood lineage continues to H.I.M. Emperor Haile Sellassie I, there can be no doubt who Sellassie I really is. Undoubtedly, Jesus Christ is truly an ancestor of Haile Sellassie I.

The "Falhashas" of Ethiopia are recorded in Ethiopian history as the people whose ancestors were the individuals from Jerusalem, who were selected by King Solomon's administrative council. They were selected to accompany King Solomon's son- Menelik I, on his return journey to Ethiopia. The Falhashas were to protect and continue the Judaic religion and education of Menelik I. To their care was endowed the Ark of the Covenant, the Judaic historic books, and other artifacts of the Solomonic era.

The Falhashas continued to live in Ethiopia up to the present time. They are known worldwide as the

"Ethiopian Jews", and are the original Jewish educators
from King David's court.

Chapter 3
JAMAICA : ITS ETHOS

"A nation without the knowledge of its past
history is like a tree without its roots."

To have a pellucid understanding of the
Rastafarian emergence in Jamaica, we must
delve into the roots and origin of the Jamaican
society. A brief history of developments in the island, will
take us along that path of human understanding which
allows a people to survive.

"Xyamaca" (pronounced Yamaca) was occupied by
the Amerindian Tribe of Arawaks in 1494, when the Nina,
Pinta, and Santa Maria sailed over its horizon and landed
with Christopher Columbus and his crew. This was perhaps the first recorded contact by Europeans and the
Arawaks. Columbus" ships were depleted of supplies.
Destitute without food, water, and hope the crew began
to rebel against the navigator. Fortunately they stumbled
upon a beautiful verdant island. The Arawaks observed
the hostility and "hooliganism" of the Spaniards, and
refused to assist them in replenishing their supplies. So
Christopher Columbus in his dire situation, devised a
plan to trick the Indians into helping him.

The story goes that Columbus remembered that
there was to be a lunar eclipse that night. He told the
Arawaks that unless they brought him food and water,
his God would be angry and would block the light of
their moon from them until they relented. The Arawaks,
superstitious and ever so cautious, still refused. Later
that night, the lunar eclipse began and the shadow crept

across the moon. A great fear enveloped the Arawaks and
they quickly brought large clay pots of water and food,
including limes, coconuts, mangoes, roast coneys, roast
pig, fish, cassava, yams, and other edibles. The eclipse
soon passed and Columbus, with his ship full of vital
supplies, sailed on ahead with a horde of Arawaks in hot
pursuit.

Years later, following Columbus' visit, the Spaniards
came in multitudes to "Xyamaca" (name given to the
island by the Arawaks meaning "the land of wood and
water"). The name was chosen for the island because of
its numerous rivers, streams, and forestry of cotton,
mahogany, mahoe, guango, and cassia trees.   The
Spaniards captured and colonized Jamaica (Xyamaca),
slaughtering the Arawaks in the process. Soon after, the
Spaniards brought in shiploads of slaves captured from
the west coast of Africa. *The slaves were used to work the
sugar plantations.*

The Spanish established Saint Jago De La Vago as the
capital city of Jamaica. The primary mountains and rivers
were renamed, among them were the Rio Cobre, Rio
Grande, Rio Minho, Rio Bueno, Mount Diablo, Mount
Pedro, Don Figuerero, and Juan De Bolas, etc.   The
Spaniards ruled Jamaica until 1665.

In 1665 the English invaded Jamaica with a mighty
armada. This force was under the joint command of
Admiral Penn and General Venables. The Spaniards fled
to Cuba with some of the slaves who fought with them
against the British invaders. Some slaves fought against
the Spaniards and remained under the English con-
querors who later colonized the island.

Under the British ruling, Port Royal became the capital city until 1692, and was the notorious home of pirates,
earning a reputation of being the "wickedest city on

earth". The notorious pirate-Sir Henry Morgan was commissioned as the first English governor of Jamaica. It
wasn't until Port Royal was destroyed by the terrible
earthquake of 1692, that Kingston became the new capital
of Jamaica. Queen Elizabeth I of England and the notorious pirate John Hawkins, established the West India Slave
Trading Company. Queen Elizabeth I bestowed knight-
hood upon John Hawkins. She commissioned a fleet of
ships to Sir John Hawkins to increase the slave trading
between Africa and the British West Indies. The flag ship
was the Slave Ship (S. S.) Jesus of Lubeck. Another was
the S. S. Zong.

Hawkins' methods of slave trading was entirely different from other slave traders. His methods were very
crude and effective. He just invaded the west coast of
Africa and seize the slaves that he needed. Those who
were captured but unwanted were instantly killed.

During the Atlantic voyage (the Middle Passage),
any slave that was ill or became weak due to severe whip-
pings and hostile conditions, was simply tossed over-
board and fed to the sharks. After much suffering and
forceful subjection to learning the English Language,
slaves were told to work until "Jesus" came. The Slaves
thought that meant S. S. Jesus of Lubeck, would return to
take them back to Africa. But the S. S. Jesus of Lubeck and
the S. S. Zong were scuttled on the Spanish Main, during
one of the wars with the Spaniards. Many slaves continued to hope for its arrival, which never came.

The slaves worked endless hours producing sugar,
molasses, rum, mined copper, built houses, and roads.
They transformed Jamaica into a salubrious resort for the
English gentry. But the British was soon to make their
first big mistake.

British slave masters concentrated a large number of

slaves from Ghana, then called the "Gold Coast". They were brought in from the Fanti and Ashanti tribes, and spoke a common language. The British named them the "Maroons". Over time they bonded and rebelled against the British. The Maroons took to the hills and mountains and won many battles over the British for decades. Led by many courageous warriors such as Cudjoe,

Quaco, and Accompong Nanny, these Ashanti natives won their independence; having a treaty signed by the British upon instruction from Queen Victoria, Sovereign of England at that time. Accompong Town became the capital for the Maroons.

August 1, 1834 Queen Victoria proclaimed the emancipation of all slaves throughout the British Empire. Queen Victoria nominated 20 million British pounds as reparation to assist the freed slaves of the Caribbean. However, the slave masters seized the money and divided it up among themselves. The ex-slaves received nothing in recompense. One could only imagine how elated the slaves were at the Proclamation of Emancipation. Some were awarded small lots of land while others were now paid a stipend for their labor.

The African slaves in Jamaica were never educated by the Spaniards and only to some extent by the English. Prior to 1834, most slaves were mainly illiterate. Now with post freedom, and faced with servicing the needs of a population overwhelmingly African, the British devised a system to keep the African-Jamaicans at the bottom of the society. They began to import immigrant workers called "indentured servants" from India and China.

The Indians were employed to maintain the sugar factories, and as proprietors of cloth, and jewelry stores. They brought with them the East Indian mangoes, the Bombay mangoes, callaloo, engentail, bal and dahl,

mango chutni, curried goat, and the renowned remarkable herb called Indian hemp or ganja" (canabis sativae).
This herb was proliferous along the banks of the
river Ganges in India. The Chinese were brought in to
establish the services of laundry, grocery, and restaurants.
They brought with them their Chinese culture, including
bok chow, chop suey, peaka pow, mahjong, and the opiate
opium.

The British enacted a law instituting that only the
Chinese were allow to sell groceries. The freed African
slaves were to be fish mongers and charcoal vendors.

During 19 century Jamaica, only the English were
allowed to vote and Jamaica was governed by an English
legislative council. The African-Jamaicans, Chinese,
Indians, and many of the English citizens bonded together and became very disenchanted with the political,
social, and economic conditions. Afro-Jamaicans held
only menial positions, mainly to plant sugarcane for the
sugar factories. There were scores of factories producing
sugar, rum, and molasses. (George Washington, first
president of the United States, used to trade slaves for
West Indian rum). Former slaves, although emancipated,
were finding it increasingly difficult to exist. Soon there
were uprisings against the British. In 1865 the Morant
Bay Rebellion was led by Deacon Paul Bogle from Stony
Gut, St. Thomas, along with Reverent George William
Gordon, a clergyman of mixed blood.

English constabulary unjustly arrested a number of
Deacon Bogle's congregation in Stony Gut. They were
tried and found guilty of sedition and instigating riots.
Paul Bogle and his parishioners then stormed the Morant
Bay Courthouse. In the ensuing battle, the custos of Saint
Thomas, Baron Von Kettleholt was killed, along with
many of the English gentry. The courthouse was burned

to the ground and many British owned properties were destroyed. The English governor called on the British troop reserve from Kingston to quell the uprising. Deacon Bogle and Reverent Gordon were captured, hastily tried, and immediately hung. The hangings did not stem the tide of the freed slave march for justice.

Other rebellions followed. There were uprisings in Saint James, the north western part of the island, where Montego Bay, its capital city, saw much turbulence. The agitation was led by a staunch non-violent leader known as Sam Sharp.

THE GARVEY ERA

At the turn of the 20th century, Marcus Mosiah Garvey rose up to inspire the people to fight for social, political, and economic changes. Marcus Garvey and Amy Ashwood co-founded the Universal Negro Improvement Association (U.N.I.A.) in 1914. He also established a printing press and was the producer of the first black owned newspaper in Jamaica. The newspaper was called *The Black Man*.

Garvey developed African fundamentalism with the creed of "One God, One Aim, One Destiny". His headquarters in Kingston was called Liberty Hall. Garvey left Jamaica and toured Cuba, Haiti, Costa Rica, and other south American countries. In 1916 he migrated to the United States of America where he launched the largest chapter of the U.N.I.A., with the headquarters in Harlem, New York. He then started a newspaper in New York called *The Negro World*.

The U.N.I.A. grew to become the largest black organization of all times, enfolding an estimated five million active members worldwide. Marcus Garvey preached that the former African slaves should be repatriated to Africa, and former slave trading countries should pay reparations for their participation in such an endeavor. His organization (U.N.I.A.) established many business enterprises to encourage black people to be independent and self-sufficient. He also founded a shipping company called the Black Star Line in 1919. These ships were used for transporting cargo and passengers all over the black world. His organization made contact and signed a lease with President King of the Republic of Liberia in 1920, for the purpose of conducting trade with the African Diaspora and repatriating people of African descent from the west who desired to return to Africa. This lease included an agreement for the people to settle on a quarter million acres of land in Liberia.

Members of the U.N.I.A. eagerly boarded the fleet of five ships from ports in the Caribbean and the United States. They loaded on seeds, grains, tractors, water pumps, tools, trucks, other equipment and materials, necessary to build a settlement in Africa. As soon as the U.N.I.A. contingent departed for Liberia, the United States government dispatched a quick light cruiser with the secretary of states on board. The cruiser sped pass the U.N.I.A.'s fleet on the high seas, landing in Liberia ahead of the U.N.I.A. fleet of ships. The United States secretary of state met with President King in a secret meeting. The contents of this meeting were never disclosed to the public. As the U.N.I.A. and its fleet approached the shores of Liberia, the Liberian Navy blocked its passage, preventing them from coming ashore. The captain of the Black Star Line sought to have a meeting with President King immediately. The U.N.I.A. displayed the lease agreement, signed and agreed upon by President King. However, President King adamantly refused to meet the

U.N.I.A. delegation.

After weeks of trying to negotiate with President King to allow the Black Star Line Crew to come ashore, and with the depletion of food and fresh water, the president of Liberia allowed only the unloading of equipment and materials from the ships. President King steadfastly refused to allow the crew to land. The equipment and materials were confiscated by the Liberian government. Eventually, Liberia's government decided to replenish the necessary supplies aboard the U.N.I.A.'s fleet of ships and instructed their navy to forcibly escort the U.N.I.A. ships out of Liberian waters.

Dejected and disappointed, the crew set sail for their return journey to the west. After crossing the Atlantic Ocean , the fleet of ships docked in Cuba. That night, the entire fleet was sabotaged and set on fire. No one was held accountable for this barbaric act. Then in 1923, Garvey was promptly arrested and charged with mail fraud and conspiracy. He was found guilty in 1925 and was sentenced to five years in prison, in the state of Georgia.

In November of 1927, Marcus Garvey was granted a pardon by President Calvin Coolidge. Upon his release from prison, Garvey was deported to Jamaica, where with his faithful lieutenants Saint William Grant, Stennett Kerr-Coombs, and others, he continued his work with the U.N.I.A. He decided to campaign for a seat on the legislative council in Jamaica. However, Garvey was arrested and found guilty of sedition. Just before sentencing, the presiding judge received a letter in chambers from the chairman of Jamaica's Council of Churches quoting "Will you Let The Tiger Loose?" When he was released from prison he left Jamaica for England, where he resided until he died in 1940.

After the Garvey era in Jamaica, Alexander Bustamante, Norman Washington Manley, Ken Hill, and other stalwarts continued the struggle for changes in Jamaica's socio-politico and economico conditions. There were riots on Kingston's water fronts, rampages on the sugar estates, and general civil disobedience by the majority of Jamaica's working class.

Bustamante founded a labor union, The Bustamante Industrial Trade Union (B.I.T.U.). Ken Hill founded the Trades Union Congress (T.U.C.). Norman Manley founded a political party called "The People's National Party" (P.N.P.). In 1938, events of civil disobedience escalated to the point where the government had no control over developments. Ensuing events caused the governor to declared a state of emergency throughout the island. Bustamante, Ken Hill, and others were arrested and detained. Bustamante was tried and convicted for sedition and was incarcerated at the governor's leisure. Eventually Bustamante was released and formed the Jamaica Labor Party (J.L.P.). Jamaica had its first universal adult suffrage vote for its government in 1944.

The Jamaica Labor Party (J.L.P.) won the elections and Sir William Alexander Bustamante became Jamaica's first chief minister and formed the first government of elected Jamaicans. Norman Manley's P.N.P. became Jamaica's first opposition party.

Chapter 4
RASTAFARI: THE DAWN

During the Marcus Garvey era (1914-1940), other important events took place in the black man's world. Garvey had taught his followers about the history of Ethiopia, Alexandria, Zimbabwe, Monomotapa, Timbuktu, Ghana, Mali, Songhai, and other great African empires of culture. He told his congregation to look to Ethiopia and the king. Subsequently the U.N.I.A.'s national anthem was, to quote a few lines:

> Ethiopia, the land of our fathers;
> The land where all Gods love to be.
> As swift bees to hive suddenly gathers;
> So thy children come rushing to thee.
> With red, yellow, and green floating 'oer us,
> And our emperor to shield us from wrong.
> With our God and our future before us;
> We hail thee with shouts and with songs!

Thus the Honorable Marcus Garvey set the stage to herald in the era of His Imperial Majesty, the Emperor Haile Sellassie I, conquering lion of the tribe of Judah. The general populace of Jamaica had felt a void with the departure and demise of the Honorable Marcus Garvey. During the 1930s, social and political strife was brewing. Saint William Grant was on the docks, organizing the labor force to unite and fight against starvation wages with no benefits.

The sugar factories were now run by giant companies (conglomerates) such as Tate and Lyle, and the West
India Sugar Company. Sugar, rum, and molasses were at
their heights, but very little benefits went to the workers.
The banks of Jamaica, as most commercial companies, did
not hire dark skinned people in any important position;
only menial jobs were available.   The United Fruit
Company controlled the growing and exportation of
bananas.

Although most of the black population was not making a decent living, a few slipped through the racial barriers and became prominently known.   Such included
barrister Ethelred Erasmus Adolphus Campbell and the
young legal wiz, barrister Norman Washington Manley.
Dr. L. Moodie, Dr. Ivan LLoyd, and young Dr. Peter Bragg
were among the few who excelled against the odds.

Disturbances were on the rise on the sugar estates all
over the island. The brothers Frank and Ken Hill, along
with Alexander Bustamante and Saint William Grant
organized the workers into unions. At this junction of
Jamaica's history, Bustamante was a member of the
People's National Party (P.N.P.); and both Norman
Manley and Bustamante were members of the Trade
Union Council. Thus, Jamaica, for the very first time, was
politically united. This was the panorama that existed
during the turbulent 1930s and early 1940s in which the
people of Jamaica were struggling to exist and to find
their true identity.

During this period, significant historic events were
also taking place in Ethiopia, on which the entire world
would soon focus. In 1916, Rastafari Makonnen, the governor of the Ethiopian province of Harrar, was proclaimed as Prince Regent and heir apparent of Ethiopia.
It was reported that the Prince Regent Rastafari

Makonnen met with Dr. Nambi Azikiwe of Nigeria, Jomo "Burning Spear" Kenyatta of Kenya, Marcus Garvey of Jamaica, and other African patriots to form the secret order of Nyabinghi. The Nyabinghi order drafted plans for the total liberation of the African continent from European domination, by any means necessary.

In 1928, Prince Regent Rastafari Makonnen was crowned as Negus (King) of Ethiopia. Then on November 2, 1930, Negus Rastafari Makonnen was crowned in Addis Ababa (the new flower), before a world audience which included England's Prince of Wales and other European royalties. He was crowned by his holiness Abuna Basilios -Patriarch of the Ethiopian Orthodox Coptic Church, as His Imperial Majesty Emperor Haile Sellassie I, Negus Negusti (king of kings), Lord of Lords, Conquering Lion of the Tribe of Judah, Lebena Denghel (incense of the virgin), Keeper of the Faith of the Dynasty of Judah, Keeper of the Faith of the Dynasty of David, and The Elect of God. Emperor Haile Sellassie was given the Golden Orb and the Golden Sceptre. Thus the coronation of His Imperial Majesty Emperor Haile Sellassie I of Ethiopia, signaled prophetically and historically, the birth of the Rastafarian movement.

In 1935, the Italian fascist dictator Benito Mussilini, ordered Italian forces under the command of Marshall Badolio, to invade Ethiopia. The troops were blessed by the Roman Catholic Pontiff before departing from Italy on their ill-fated adventure.

The invasion of Ethiopia by Italy, twice in a span of forty years (1896 and 1935), was the catalyst which focused "Garveyites" (followers of Marcus Garvey) and other black people on Ethiopia and His Imperial Majesty Emperor Haile Sellassie I. The culmination of events occurring in Ethiopia during the 1930s and the military

developments in Europe (World War 11), were the cata-
lysts which created the spawn for the Rastafarian dawn.

Chapter 5
CONCEPTS OF THE RASTAFARIAN

From the study of the Holy Bible, the history of man on earth and the universal love of mankind, and since Almighty God has placed on limitations no man's faculties, the Rastafarian brethren have derived their conceptions based upon the divinity of His Imperial Majesty Emperor Haile Sellassie I. All Rastafarian brethren hold sacred three basic concepts of the culture, to which we offer biblical and historical concordance; particularly the recorded history of Ethiopia.

"CONCEPTIONS"

1) That H.I.M. Emperor Haile Sellassie I of Ethiopia is the returned Messiah, the God Head, the Ancient of Days.

2) That all the African peoples brought to the west ern hemisphere through the advent of European slave trading, whose progeny still survives, have the inherent rights to demand their repatriation back to the African continent if so desired. All costs and reparations should be contributed by nations that participated in the nefarious practice of African slave trading.

3) That Ethiopia is an integral part of the Garden of Eden, as recorded in the book of Genesis.

"Biblical and Historical Concordance"

1) On the November 2, 1930, the Prince Regent Rastafari Makonnen of Ethiopia was crowned as H. I. M. Emperor Haile Sellassie I, King of Kings, Lords of Lords, Conquering Lion of the tribe of Judah, Incense of the Virgin, Keeper of the Faith of the Dynasty of Judah, Keeper of the Faith of the Dynasty of David, and the Elect of God. The significance of the name Haile Sellassie means the power of the trinity.

Emperor Haile Sellassie I is the 225th king in lineage to King Solomon and the Queen of Sheba. This ancestry is of direct descent from King David and the Queen Bathsheba (3,500 B.C.) H.I.M. Emperor Haile Sellassie I, traces his dynasty to Kush (6,500 B.C.), and beyond that to Ori (10,000 B.C.) prior to recorded European civilization. Emperor Haile Sellassie I is the 66th king of Ethiopia of the House of Judah since the 13th century restoration.Saint Matthew Chapter 1-"The genealogy from Abraham to Jesus Christ." Psalm 97, verse 1- "The Lord reigneth; let the earth rejoice; let the multitude of isles be glad thereof. "

Revelations Chapter 5, verse 5- "And one of the elders saith unto me weep not; behold the Lion of the Tribe of Judah, the root of David, hath prevailed to open the book and loose the seven seals thereof. "

Revelations Chapter 17, verse 14- "These shall wage war with the lamb, but the lamb shall overcome them for he is Lord of Lords and King of Kings."

Revelations Chapter 19, verse 16- "And he hath on his vesture and on his thigh a name written Kings of Kings and Lord of Lords."

Revelations Chapter 22, verse 16- "I am the root and the offspring of David, and the bright and morning star."

2) The history of European nations trading African slaves to the western hemisphere is well recorded in history. The scattering and gathering of the African slaves are prophesied in the scriptures.

Isaiah Chapter 43, verses 5 to 7- "Fear not for I am with thee, I will bring thy seed from the east and gather thee from the west. I will say unto the north, give up, and to the south keep not back. Bring my sons from far, and my daughters from the ends of the earth, even everyone that is called by my name. " Rastafari!

Isaiah Chapter 49, verse 1- "Listen O isles unto me; and harken ye people from far. The Lord hath call me from the womb; from the bowels of my mother (Africa) hath He made mention of my name." Rastafari!

Isaiah Chapter 51, verse 5- "My righteousness is near; my salvation is gone forth, and my arms shall judge the people. The isles shall wait upon me and on my arm shall they trust."

Isaiah Chapter 60, verse 9- "Surely the isles shall wait for me, and the ships of tarshish first, to bring thy sons from far. Their silver and their gold with them unto the name of the Lord thy God, unto the Holy one of Israel, because He hath glorified them."

Hebrews Chapter 11, verse14- "And they that say such things declare plainly that they seek a country; and truly if they had been mindful of that country from whence they came out, they might have had opportunity to have returned."

It is written that princes shall come out of Egypt, Ethiopia shall stretch forth her hands unto God. It is also written "Are thee not like the Ethiopians unto me; O ye children of Israel?"

3) Genesis Chapter 2, verses 10 to 14- "And a river

went out of Eden to water the garden; and from thence it was parted, and became into four heads. The name of the first is Pison; that is it which compasseth the whole land of Havilah, where there is gold. And the gold of that land is good; there is bdellium and the Onyx stone. And the name of the second river is Gihon; the same is it that compasseth the whole land of Ethiopia. And the name of the third river is Hiddekel; that is it which goeth towards the east of Assyria. And the fourth river is Euphrates."

Isaiah Chapter 43, verse 3- "For I am the Lord thy God, the Holy One of Israel; thy Savior. I gave Egypt for thy ransom, Ethiopia and Seba for thee."

Ethiopia is the cradle of mankind's civilization; indeed Ethiopia is the only existing country in the world since recorded history with its continuous original name, location, peoples and ethos, which has existed throughout the millennium to the present times. These three concepts mentioned above, are the ties that bind the Rastafarian brotherhood.

Since Ethiopia has the longest and earliest continuous biblical recorded history of any nation on this planet earth, that caused successive Italian military invasion, blessed by the Roman Catholic Pontiff, to suppress Ethiopian authenticity of recorded facts of history and biblical liturgy. These invasions by the Italians, were deliberate attempts to destroy and obliterate the lineage of the Solomonic Dynasty; perpetuated by progeny to H.I.M. Emperor Haile Sellassie I. Both incursions failed miserably as prophesized in the book of Revelations "That these shall make war with the lamb, but the lamb shall overcome them, for He is King of Kings and Lord of Lords."

One can ponder the consequences if the Italians had succeeded in their nefarious plot. Ethiopia by name, would have been erased. This was evident during the period of 1935-1941, when Italy having occupied only a small part of Ethiopia, began to rename the country as Abbysinia.

Being the only black country that had never been conquered or colonized by European empires, Ethiopia was the pride and the shining light for all black people universally.

In 1896 at the battle of Adowa, Emperor Menelik II and his Ethiopian forces crushed the invading Italian forces, inflicting a humiliating defeat upon their forces.

This was the first recorded victory of an African country over any European country. Having thus languished under the pangs of such a rout, Italy under the fascist dictator Benito Mussolini, again invaded Ethiopia in 1935, occupying the capital, Addis Ababa and some other areas. At no time did the invading Italians conquer the entire country; and for six long years there were continuous battles.

In 1936 the Emperor Haile Sellassie I leading an Ethiopian delegation, made a personal appeal to the League of Nations at the emergency conference in Geneva. Emperor Haile Sellassie I asked the assembled nations to assist Ethiopia with arms as a mean of allowing Ethiopia to defend themselves against the genocidal aggression of Italy. All the European nations in the League of Nations voted against Ethiopia's request. The only exceptions were the United States of America and Japan. After the vote, denying Ethiopia any military assistance, Emperor Haile Sellassie I addressed the council, telling them "That God and history would remember your judgment, if you do not bow before these accomplished facts. You have struck the match in Ethiopia, but it shall burn Europe."

How prophetic were the Emperor's words that in 1938 Benito Mussolini forged an alliance with Adolph Hitler. The united nazi and fascist forces unleashed their destructive fury upon Europe, thereby engulfing the entire world in the largest expanse of military aggression ever witnessed by mankind. (WW II). Over sixty million people were killed during this great war before it ended in 1945.

In 1941, with Italian forces poised to capture the Suez Canals, England decided to assist Ethiopia. Now with the arms and military assistance of the British led by General Wingate, Ethiopian patriots, under the command of H.I.M. Emperor Haile Sellassie I, crushed the Italian occupying forces, liberating Ethiopia and the Red Sea area. (Revelations Chapter 17, verse 14 came to pass).

From that point on (1941), the allied forces marched from victory to victory, finally crushing the axis forces (1945). The people of the world were finally liberated from the heels of nazism, fascism, and nipponism.

During an interview in Addis Ababa in 1947, Emperor Haile Sellassie I gave this speech to a panel of American journalists : "We in Ethiopia have one of the oldest version of the Bible. But however old the version may be, or in whatever language it may be written, the words remain one and the same. Today, man sees all his hopes and aspirations crumble, he is perplexed and knoweth not wither he is drifting; but he must realize that the Bible is his refuge. In it he will find a source of infinite comfort and joy: "Come unto me all ye that labor and are heavily laden and I will give thee rest". Who could resist an invitation so full of compassion?

I, from my early childhood, have been taught to appreciate the Bible and its great message. Therefore I caused a new translation (from Geez to Amharic) into a language which the young and the old understood and spoke. And that by reading the Bible, they can find truth for themselves. For my part, I glory in the Bible."

This eulogy of H.I.M. Emperor Haile Sellassie I, is typical of the Messiah giving verbal comfort to universal mankind. Indeed, no other head of state had ever spoken so emphatically to address humanity's troubled minds, giving counsel and guidance.

The messianic pertinence of the Emperor Haile Sellassie I is noticeable whenever he addresses the international press. In 1963 while addressing the United Nation's general assembly in New York, His Imperial Majesty said "Until the philosophy that makes one race superior and another inferior, is finally and permanently discredited and abandoned; until there is no longer second class citizens of any nation; until the color of a man's skin is of no more significance than the color of his eyes; until the basic human rights are guaranteed to all without regard to race; until that day the dream of international morality and lasting peace will be but a fleeting illusion to be pursued, but never attained; and until that day the earth shall know no peace." "We Africans are prepared to fight if necessary and we know that we shall win because we are confident in the triumph of good over evil."

The significance of these prophetic words cannot escape mankind's attention. There can be no basis of peace on earth without justice and equality to all mankind. Is there any other head of state who had ever so nobly spoken on the brotherhood of man before the world? Emperor Haile Sellassie I was the ultimate philosophical philanthropist.

The preceding analogies should provide an analytical thesis to the thoughts of Rastafarian concepts, based upon the divinity of His Imperial Majesty Emperor Haile

Sellassie I.

Chapter 6
THE CAMPS

During the 1930s, the Honorable Marcus Garvey's motto of "One God, one aim, and one destiny" burned in the heart of every black Jamaican. That motto was the inspiration to rise above the dark clouds of colonialism. In Ethiopia, the coronation of His Imperial Majesty Emperor Haile Sellassie as Negus Negusti, and Ambassa Ye Huda, signaled the joy of a new beginning to the African Diaspora throughout the western hemisphere. One can only imagine the ecstasy and joy that such an event brought to the souls of former slaves; to see an African so universally exalted, even by the very powers that suppressed black people's aspirations during that era.

The 1935 invasion of Ethiopia by Benito Mussolini's Italian forces and the reported savagery perpetrated against the Ethiopian people galvanized the people of African descent throughout the entire world. Over five hundred thousand Ethiopian patriots were murdered by the fascist army. Indeed that single act by Italy awakened the universal conscience of all African people and exposed Europe's intention to erase the kingdom of man's earliest civilization. Italy's intent was to capture Ethiopia's precious artifacts and to eradicate black Judeo-Christian history, embodied in the Solomonic Dynasty continuance through the lineage of Emperor Haile Sellassie I. The rise of Rastafarian camps throughout Jamaica derived from these events arose consciousness.

Knowing that Ethiopia educated the Greeks, who later educated the Romans, must have been a bitter pill to swallow for white supremacy egotism. In Greek mythology Perseus, a prince of Greece who slew the Medusa, was married to the Ethiopian princess Andromeda. A star in our galaxy was later named Andromeda after her.

Brother Leonard Percival Howell was the first recorded Rastafarian brethren who openly preached the divinity of H.I.M. Emperor Haile Sellassie I, as the returned Messiah, the Godhead in the flesh. Brother Howell eventually established a large Rastafarian camp and self sustained community called "Pinnacle" in the parish of Saint Catherine, in the hills near Sligoville. He was revered in the Rastafarian community and his word was "law" in Pinnacle. A council of elders was established to assist in the daily administration of the camp, and to maintain discipline among the brethren who dwelt there. The camp of Pinnacle expanded to embrace hundreds of brethren, some who resided and some who were frequent visitors.

Some of the residing brethren I recalled, were Brother Panty Ossie, Brother Ram, Brother Sterling "The Blind", Brother Lover, and Brother Joshi. The brethren all had their queens and children all living around the community. They planted plenty of crops such as banana, yam, peas, sweet potato, tampi, cocoa, corn and plantain. Natural herbs were also grown. They reared chicken, cows, goats, horses, and donkeys. The brethren were self sustained and self employed. They made slippers from old automobile tires which they called "Power". The scarves they made were weaved in the Rastafarian colors of red, yellow, and green (red, gold, and green). They also made mats, baskets, hats and other items from straw. Rope and cord were made from sisal and hemp which they planted; and they also burned charcoal. The ware and produce were sold in the surrounding areas of

Spanish Town and to frequent Pinnacle visitors.

The large gathering of brethren at Pinnacle, together with the crops of "Cannabis Sativae" called Ganja, tampi, or herb, which was used in the religious rites and also sold to visitors, were the excuses used by the police to carry out frequent raids on Pinnacle. Brother Howell often rode his horse around the community from time to time in order to inspect the crops and camp activities. Brethren would run, following his horse, anywhere he went. The community became prosperous and Brother Howell became very "well off". Brother Howell had two sons who grew up on Pinnacle - Monty and Blade. Blade was nicknamed "Gong".

During one of the police (Babylon) raids on Pinnacle, Brother Howell was arrested and sent to prison for cultivating Ganja. Upon his release, he returned to Pinnacle where he continued his activities. It was rumored that his queen (one of his wives at common law) was pregnant with another brother's baby while he was away. It was alleged that a council of elders tried her for adultery, she was found guilty and subsequently stoned from Pinnacle, and she never returned.

Another community of brethren, closely affiliated with Pinnacle, developed in the Jones Pen area of Saint Catherine. Among those brethren were Father Roe, Brother Son, Brother Jazzbo, and Brother Presley. Pinnacle thrived as a Rastafarian community for decades until 1954 when Brother Howell's "nemesis" Detective Inspector Jez Marston, accompanied by hundreds of police officers in trucks, jeeps, horsebacks, and foot, carried out a massive and extensive raid on Pinnacle which lasted for several days.

Scores of brethren were arrested, mainly on Ganja cultivating charges. The camp, homes, and hundred of acres of crops were burned and destroyed. The fires and destruction were so extensive that for nearly a week Ganja smoke, dust, ash, and other debris rained down and blanketed Spanish Town and nearby surrounding areas. People were coughing and gasping for days.

That infamous raid devastated the Rastafarian community and Pinnacle was never the same again. The brethren scattered, settling primarily in Kingston, St. Andrew, and St. Catherine areas. Thus Inspector Jez Marston's action had the positive reaction of expanding the Rastafarian camp, rather than the anticipated demise of the culture. The Rastafarian brethren began to establish camps all over the corporate areas by the mid 1940s after the second world war.

Brother Lover was one of Brother Howell's disciples who left Pinnacle during the 1940s and came to establish his own camp on the long mountain road area of Warieka Hills. This road is now known as Mountain View Avenue. Some of Brother Lover's followers were Brother Joshi, Count Ossie, Brother Job, Josiah, Brother Careful, Brother Richard, and Brother Phil. Brother Job was the master Akete drummer at that time.

Count Ossie later established his own camp off Windward Road, opposite Slip Dock Road. A large following of brethren assembled around Count Ossie's camp where Count now started to beat his own drums. Some of his followers were Brother Phil, Brother Paddy Knox "The Baron", Ras Daniel, Bongo Saulanka, Izzie Boat, Brother Seiges, Leighton "Worm", Paddy Whiskey, Big Jeff Folks, Brother Jari Boots "Beck", Brother Nuxie, Brickie "The Fox", Guzzu Warrior, The Rumpel, Uttus, Brother Huey "The B.A.", Little John Mistic, Big Ben, Brother Mario, Brother Teekis, Brother Bygo "The Guitarist", Jah Jerry, Brother White "The Saxman", "The

Vocalist" Fred Stanley, Brother Tami, and Big Bra Gaynair. Big Bra and the other musicians frequently rehearsed their music and were backed up by the beat of Count Ossie's African drums.

The 1951 storm "Hurricane Charlie" devastated Jamaica and Count Ossie relocated his camp to Adastra Road in the Rennock Lodge area of Warieka Hills. Many more were attracted to the camp and the brotherhood grew. Along with its original members, the camp included men such as Don Drummond, Brother Balboa, John Tinker, Brother

Squall, Brother Steretts, Brother Woody, Smoke Stack, Rico Tingling, Rico Trombone, Bunny and Skitter "The Singers", Dizzy Johnny, Peanuts, John Buggs, Brother Stove, Ronnie McFish, Earl "Apache", Brother Roy-yo, Little Bra, Little Bop, and Strato. It was on Count Ossie's camp, backed up by Count's African drums, that the Folks brothers first rehearsed a song that was later recorded as "O Carolina". This recording made Count Ossie famous.

After Count Ossie left the Windward Road area, Guzzu Warrior and the Rumpel took over that camp. The brothers that assembled there now included Brother Jay Slow, Brother Shakey, Brother Stanford, China Vinny, Big Beard John, and Big Boy. The camp was renamed "Seoul".

Poker Flat brethren included Brother Powdie, Brother Roy "Rider", Lion Heart, Brother Gussie, Bongo Spree Boy, Bongo Zekel, Palueky, The Scaramouche, Brother Bravo, Brother Kirton, Brother Baboo, Crasher, Brother Louie, Buttie Green and Brother Roy.

Brother Beeky's camp, where I used to frequent, consisted of Brother Tin Pan, Brother Tally, Tall Ossie, Brother Chilly, Big Dike, Brother B.G., Brother Dantes,

Brother Willow, Brother Sleezy, Brother Quitty, Balti Lowe, and Brother Raca "Israel".

Brother Larry's brethren included Little Ossie, Brother Lloydie, Brother Con, Little Shaggie, Bongo Freddie, Bongo Sil, John Bull, and Sister Winnie. Paradise Street's brethren included Brother Chummy, Brother Tarsha, Bulla Rim, Brother Byron, Brother Scabbo, Brother Junior, Bailey Boy, and Brother Humpy.

Mountain View Hillside's brethren were Baba Boab, Big Steel, Brother Siddi, Brother Chana, Brother Exell, Brother Spunky and Brother Roy, the shoe maker.

Brother Skipper's camp was located on the dungle behind the Coronation Market, on lands known as "Back-o'-Wall". Assembled with Brother Peter "Skipper" were Brother Planno, Brother Napier, Wolfman, Brother Tull, Brother Ken Frasier, Brother Scully, Brother Danny "Donkey Man", Brother Color Red, Brother Spence and Bongo Watto.

The brethren, along with Brother Skipper, established the first local branch (37) of the Ethiopian World's Federation Inc. in Jamaica.

Maxfield Park's brethren consisted of Brother Qutang, Brother Tex, and Brother Caleb.

Brother Sallo's Waterhouse brethren included Brother Baugh, Brother Baker, Big D, Upsweep, Ras Walt Phillips, Big Manus, Brother McKonnen, and Sister Baugh. Clock Circle and Ghost Town brethren were Brother Eric, Brother Duffus, Brother Huey, Brother Pic, Brother Neville, Jeweler John, Bongo Herman, Brother Ritchie, and Brother Jackie.

The Jones Town brethren consisted of Brother Phantom, Brother Simmo "Swami", Brother Myrie, and Brother Flampie.

The Foreshore Road and Greenish Farm brethren were Brother Watta King, Brother Sam Brown, Coolie Boy, Chuchi, Bongo Meshach, Bongo Shadrach, and Bongo Abednego.

Ackee Walk's camp along Spanish Town Road., was established by Prince Emmanuel and his brethren. The police constantly harassed these brethren. Eventually there was an inflagration in 1960 during a Rastafarian convention at Prince Emmanuel's camp. Over ninety Rastafarian brethren were arrested, including Prince Emmanuel. Due to the disturbance, the University of the West Indies sent out a team of investigators to various Rastafarian camps, especially in the corporate areas. After their fact findings, the University of the West Indies made some recommendations to the Jamaican government. The recommendations included the following:

a) Most Rastafarians were peaceful and posed no threat to others.
b) They should not be discriminated against in the work force because of their unshaven features.
c) The government should send a fact finding team of delegates to Africa to investigate the possibility of a "Back to Africa Movement".

The Tower Street brethren included Brother Menelik, Brother Crackie, Brother Kettol, and Brother Dixie "The Vocalist".

Brother Brown of Montego Bay, established a large camp and business enterprise. This included a bakery, furniture and craft store, and a grocery store. The brethren also established a branch of the Ethiopian World Federation Inc.

Custos Kerr Jarrett of the parish of Saint James, sent Brother Brown as a delegate to a convention of "moral rearmament" being held in the United States.

Rastafarians islandwide, rejected the "moral rearmament" as Euro-caucasian brain washing.

Glendevon and Granville in the Montego Bay area, were also sites of large Rastafarian camps. I visited these brethren on many occasions.

There were many other camps scattered over the island; but the above mentioned camps are some of the original established from1930 to 1950. I was personally acquainted with all these brethren, with whom I frequently reasoned on Rastafarian concepts and philosophies.

The camps were the places of retreat from Babylonian pressures of life, where we acquired our spiritual meditation. We became avid scholars of the Bible, reading, reasoning, and interpreting the passages while chanting our songs of praises to the "Most High". The spirit of the camp created a soothing balm to the aching soul. Our philosophy of life meant living the physical and spiritual according to the dictates of the Scriptures, not as the Babylonian world demanded. Cleanliness meant Godliness within and out. To be a Rastafarian meant to abide by the ten commandments. The biblical scriptures were our guide, to be applied with reason to the physical frailties of mankind's everyday existence.

The brethren congregated to participate in group readings of the Bible, various history books, news papers, magazines, and other literature. The contents of these readings were discussed until we arrived at a consensus. This consensus would be communicated and debated from one camp to the other, until we reached a oneness of purpose.

Activities varied from camp to camp as brethren pursued their livelihood. Most brethren were highly skilled tradesmen and were self-employed. Some were plumbers, cabinet makers, auto mechanics, wood carvers, knitters, fishermen etc. Few held jobs in other people's established businesses.

Leading up to 1960, Rastafarians were ostracized by the established societal employers. Very few hired Rastafarians, and one would be fired if he became a converted Rastafarian while being employed. Grounds for being fired included growing one's hair, and speaking about Africa and the divinity of Emperor Haile Sellassie I.

I distinctly remember one day in 1955, in my uncle's home at Sheffield Road, where there was a family gathering, when all the conversation seemed to be focused on me (my Rastafarian lifestyle was being discussed and disputed). I told my relatives that I would live to see the day when every single country on the African continent would be free from European colonization and become free independent states. At that time only Ethiopia and Liberia were independent African states. One of my uncles stated that I was mad and that I would never live to see that day. I reiterated that not only would all of Africa be free in my lifetime, but I was also going to see man landing on the moon. The next day, my uncle sent for Dr. Royes, a prominent psychiatrist, to interview and assess my mental state. After a lenthy discussion between Dr. Royes and myself, in the presence my relatives, Dr. Royes assured them that not only was I of sound mind and body but that I was an extremely intelligent and knowledgeable person. The doctor advised them not to ostracize me because of my religious beliefs, but to extend any assistance that I needed if they could afford to.

I left my home that day to visit my brethren on a

camp, smiling all the way. I felt fully vindicated and elated. Time now shows that my prognostications were correct. My uncle witnessed all these predictions fulfilled
before his demise.

The Republic of Ghana gained independence from
Britain just 18 months after my conversations with Dr.
Royes. And man and machines have since landed on the
moon.

During the turbulent period of 1961, when the
Rastafarian brethren were being bombarded by the
Jamaican institutional society, Brother Phil and I rode our
bicycles all over the corporate areas, making frequent
daily visits to all the camps mentioned. We consulted and
reasoned with the brethren to establish cohesion, conti-
nuity, and self reliance, in lieu of Babylon's continued
ostracism. Frequent raids and arrests on "framed up"
charges were the order of the day. Many brethren were
forcibly shaved by the police.

Still, through all these trying times, our brethren
stood close to each other. The love, unity, and communal
spirit that existed among us, made us weather the storm.
"Bear ye one another's burden and so fulfill the law of
Christ."

The brothers who were fisherman (and there were
many), would fish all night, sell most of the catch, and
bring the rest to the camp. The same held true for the
peanut and other vendors. We all donated tithes from our
labors toward the general welfare of our brethren. This
was how life was on the camps.

In 1960 I transferred my camp from Windward Road
to a section of Warieka Hills just off Glasspole Avenue.
The brethren assembled around me were Jah Monty, Big
Dyke, Brother Shaggy, Brother Moses, Brother Sam,
Brother Calvin, Brother Con, Brother Ramie "Bishop",

Brother Touy, Brother Persian, Brother Manny, Brother Dantes, Brother Winston "Rockie", Brother Berris, Brother Smoke Stack, Brother Morgie, Brother Raki, Brother Zuki, Brother Vernon " The Prophet", Brother Mouzie, and Brother Phil. As a group we read various world wide publications. The Ethiopian Times and World News, published by Dr. Richard Pankhurst in London, was the chief source of information for us from the late 1930's to the early 1960's. During the 1950's I would often get my Ethiopian Times from an elder brethren named Brother Menelik from Tower Street. The Ethiopian Times gave us a lot of current information on events taking place in Ethiopia. It informed us of Ethiopia's war with Italy, the counter attacks of the Ethiopian patriots, Ethiopia's raids on the Italians led by Ras Kassa, Ras Imru, Ras Desta and others, and the military exploits of His Imperial Majesty on the battle field.

This newspaper often published graphic photographs of Italian atrocities. I can still remember how shocked I was to see photographs of Italian soldiers laughing while they held aloft, or lined up on a stone wall, the severed heads of bearded Ethiopian patriots. Indeed, if not for Dr. Pankhurst's Ethiopian Times, these atrocities would not have been known to the outside world.

Brother Menelik was the first brethren to communicate with the Ethiopian Orthodox Church in British Guyana in the early 1940's. Abba Gebre Sellassie was the priest who responded to Brother Menelik's letters. Brother Menelik was one of my early mentors.

In the mid 1950's Counselor Peter Evans, an Englishman, established a book store below his office on Tower Street, where the brethren could get weekly Ethiopian Times edition. Counselor Evans was declared "persona non gratia" after he helped to defend 90 brethren who were arrested in the aftermath of the riots of 1960, in the Ackee Walk area of Spanish Town Road.

Dr. Pankhurst and his wife Sylvia were honored by H.I.M. Emperor Haile Sellassie I for their contribution of literary work on Ethiopia, after the war with Italy ended.

It was from my camp in Warieka Hills that Brother Phil and I left that morning in April of 1961 to join other delegates on the first historic mission to five African countries.

THE RASTAFARIAN SISTERS

"I am black but comely as the tents of Kedar, as
the curtains of Solomon."
                    (Song of Solomon, Chapter 1, verse 5)

The camps were the foundation for acquiring knowledge of the Rastafarian philosophy. Although all the brethren were affiliated with individual camps, some lived outside the camps with their wives or their queens.

Behind the scene of activity were the daughters of Zion, the Rastafarian sisters, each resolute in defense of her kingman. Some of the daughters embraced the philosophy with fervor and zeal, while others were satisfied just to be with their kingmen. The sisters were a tower of strength in the daily activities on the camps. Among the domestic chores, they were also responsible for educating the children, because some brethren were against educating their children by the "Babylonian Methods." The daughters even assisted in confronting the police whenever they raided the camps. Some policemen were trigger happy and displayed forceful animosity towards the brethren, but were cautious and quiet when confronted by the daughters. The women were also needed to obtain bail for a brother who was incarcerated; usually for possession of ilee (marijuana). They knew how to use their feminine charm to persuade officers to drop the charges.

Rastafarians' idrens had a hard time getting room and board for their families outside of the camps. To get around this, they would send the daughters to negotiate the rent or lease with the owner. If successful, the women and children would occupy the premises before the brother could make an appearance. Many times when the owners became aware of the situation they would give an immediate notice to vacate. At times, the women would lease a lot of land. The family of this property would then call the other brethren to assist them in erecting a wood house. This would incite a groundation to formally christen the premises.

The Rastafarian sisters who frequented the camps in the late 1940's and 1950's were from various areas. The sisters from Slip Dock Road, Count Ossie's first camp, were Sisters Pam, Shirley 'Needle,' Jennie, Katherine, and brother Lover's queen with the beard, Sister Daphne. Queen Baby I from Ackee Walk and Sister Puncee from Clarendon were on the scene. The daughters from Ghost Town were Sisters Dell, Angie, Joyce, Gloria and Madgi. From Count Ossie's relocated camp at Rennock Lodge came Sisters Sweeny, Daphne, Joyce, Dotty, Baby Lov, Mary and Sister Consie. The Poker Flat crew were Mother Julie, sisters Tiny, Wilda, Blossom, Barbara, Maudie, Cynthia, Madge, Winnie, Queenie from Mountain View, Red Top and Joyce from Tower Street. From Glaspole Avenue in Warieka Hills, where my camp was based, included Sisters Shuggus, Sissie Maybel, Daisy, Big Cynthia, Panzie, Topsie, Mother Theresa, Margaritta, Ruby Juvenile, and Audrey who became my wife and the

mother of my children. There were many other Rasta
Sister, however these women were pioneers and support-
ed the culture with vigor.

The socio-economical conditions of Jamaica during
the 1950's were designed to oppress the Jamaican of
African descent. As a result, this stimulated the growth of
the Rastafarian movement. The younger generation were
looking for an alternative life style to that of their parents.
The root of the Rastafarian life style was to embrace and
promote the African culture. The organization of the
camps were modern renditions of the villages in the
mother land. The brethren's attire was the dashiki, which
they thought was more suitable for the Caribbean climate. The sisters in their own right, were trend setters.
Rastafarians believed that women should exude their
femininity at all times. The sisters weren't encouraged to
wear pants, make-up or straighten their hair. To accentu-
ate their looks without indulging in the Babylonian standard of beauty, they adorned themselves with head raps,
long skirts or dresses made from colorful kente cloth.
Many women would sport low hair, which during this
time in Jamaica was not an acceptable look for the populace. The constant images of the Rastafarian sistren re-
enforced the beauty of black women in the Jamaican society. Great evidence of this was in the reggae music. Black
women were referred to as African Queens. They were
praised for their natural unspoiled beauty. The society
was being remolded. A woman's beauty was no longer
measured by the European standard.

Because of political circumstances and prejudice
toward the Rastafarian man, it was easier for the women
to gain employment. Many sisters became the main
breadwinner in the family. The sisters from the rural
areas would teach the brothers how to cultivate crops to

sell at the market. Other sisters would weave tams, hats and mats from wool and straw to gain income. A few of the women were performers. Sister Margarita was an outstanding singer and dancer. Sisters Shuggus and Maudie were dancers with Count Ossie and The African Drums.

I must commend the Daughters of Zion for standing beside us so valiantly; never wavering, even though there were tremendous pressure on each of them.

RASTAFARIAN CHANTS

The Blackman's Universal National Anthem written by the Honorable Marcus Garvey

Eternal thou God of the Ages
Grant unto thy sons that lead
thy wisdom thou gave to the sages
when Israel was sore in need.

Thy voice through the dim past has spoken.
Ethiopia shall stretch forth her hands
By thee shall all Barriers be broken
and heaven help our Dear Father's Land

Chorus: Advance. Advance to victory
                Let Africa be Free
                To Advance to meet the Foes
                To Advance to meet the Foes
                With Righteousness leading
                We haste to the call
                Humanity's pleading
                One God For us all.

Ethiopia the Land of our Fathers
The Land where all God's Love to be,
As swift bees to hive
Suddenly Gather
Thy children come rushing to thee
with the red-gold-and green
Floating o'er us
And our Emperor to shield us from wrong
With our God and Our Future before us
We hail thee with shouts and with song.

Chorus: Advance, Advance, etc

Ehtiopia the Tyrants are fallen
Who smote thee upon thy knees
And thy children are lustily calling
From over the distant seas.
Jahovah the Great One has heard us
He has heard our cries and our tears,
With the Spirit of Love he has taught us
To be one through the coming years.

Chorus: Advance, Advance to Victory. etc.

Rally to Red Gold and Green

Come rally to red gold and green
Hands and hearts must be pure
and be clean
For the key must be sincerity
with Justice and Equality.
Equality cometh for all
All who know Satan's Kingdom must Fall
For the Father hath sent us a son
To break down their swords and their guns.
No matter what powers there be
Can Prevent Emperor Haile Sellassie
For the Lion of Judah is here
To Give every one equal share.

Never to be Remembered anymore
Never to be remembered anymore
Cast your record of sinfulness
into the sea of forgetfulness
Never to be remembered anymore.

Universal Tribulation

Universal Tribulation
is upon mankind
see the people disunited in this time.
Come together, Brother. Sister.
Time is gliding on
Hear the voice of Ethiopia
Everyone.
Emperor Haile Sellassie
Hail the King of Time
They say Jesus we say Negus
True birthright.
Enemies of Ethiopia
Must go down in One.
There shall never be another.
Babylon!

I Want to See King Rastafari

I want to see King Rastafari
To Look upon His Face,
with the sheets of glory, shining around his face.
I want to bid all the gentiles them to come,
to look upon his face.
Going home, we'are going home
To see King Rasta's Face.

Chorus. Ally ally ally ally
ally lu yaa
ally ally ally ally
ally lu yaa
ally ally ally ally
ally lu yaa
ally lu yaa

For Negus is the Rock of Ages
Cleft For "I"
For Negus is the Rocks of Ages
Cleft For "I"
For Negus is the Rocks of Ages
Cleft For "I"
Ally Lu Yaa

Peace and Love

Peace and Love
Peace and Love
Peace and Love I leave with you
Peace and Love

If your Brother won't come
If your Brother won't come
Peace and Love you leave with him,
Peace and Love.

If your Sister won't come
If your Sister won't come
Peace and Love you leave with her
Peace and Love.

Holy Mount Zion
Holy Mount Zion
Holy Holy Holy Holy Holy
Holy Holy Mount Zion.
Rastafari come from Mount Zion
Rastafari come from Mount Zion
Holy Holy Holy Holy Holy
Holy Holy Mount Zion
Rastaman ah go ah Mount Zion
Rastaman ah go ah Mount Zion
Holy Holy Holy Holy Holy Holy Holy
Holy Mount Zion.

You Can Count on I

You can count on I
Working for King Rastafari
Faithful I will be
I will Fight Babylon
with all my might
You can count on me,
"Repeat" 3 times.

By The Rivers of Babylon

By the Rivers of Babylon
Where we sat down
And there we wept
When we remember Zion
For the wicked carried us away in capitivity
Required from us a song
But how can we sing
Rastafari Song in a Strange Land
Repeat three times.

Chapter 7

GROUNDATION

To understand the fundamentals and circulation of the Rastafarian culture one has to probe into the era of pre-independent Jamaica, specifically the period of 1930 to 1962. It was during this time that historic world events occurred in sequence and fused with the prophecies written in the King James Authorized Version of the Bible.

European Judeo -Christian religion was taught and fervently embedded into the minds of the Jamaican populace by our British task masters. These teachings developed a psyche, allowing us to interpret specific events according to that which was prophesied. Hence, in 1930 H. I.M. coronation as the King of Kings, together with the 1935 invasion of Ethiopia by Italy, clarified the prophesy recorded in the book of Revelations, Chapter 17. "These shall wage war with the lamb, but the lamb shall overcome them, for He is King of Kings and Lord of Lords." Thus in 1941 H.I.M. Haile Sellassie crushed the Italian forces. (The lamb overcame them). In retrospect those events were the spectra which precipitated the advent of the Rastafarian movement.

One by one brethren assembled on camps daily for the everyday activities of the culture. Occasionally a "Groundation" was held for special events. A Groundation was an all day, all night celebration, when brethren would assemble at a particular camp for a special occasion. For instance, on November 2nd which was the coronation anniversary of His Imperial Majesty

Emperor Haile Sellassie I, New Year's eve night to ring in
the new year, August 1st - Emancipation Day, and other
special occasions. These events were celebrated by the
Rastafarians long before Jamaica gained independence.

At Groundation brethren came to get acquainted
with other brethren in an atmosphere to lighten and live-
ly up one's self. Brothers sat in a circle with the "chalice
of herb" (Cutchie or Chillum pipe) being passed on the
left hand side; the left hand being closest to the heart.
This herb called Ganja was chosen to be used because it
was reportedly seen growing out of King Solomon's
grave. Hence the pseudonym "Wisdom weed". This
weed became a part of Rastafarian religious rituals.

Groundation included the recital of prayers, poems,
chanting of songs and biblical passages. The beating of
the Akete (drums) was an integral part of the Rastafarian
chanting. The set of drums were comprised of a repeater,
the Fundahs, and a bass. Usually there were at least three
Fundahs which provided the steady rhythm. The
repeater provided a Stacatto variety in tone and pitch,
while the bass provided a steady sonic reverberation, producing a confluence of systematic vibrations pleasing to
the ear. Brethren would dance around the Akete and
when the vibrations peaked, there would be shouts of
lightning and thunder in unison, as if to invoke the power
of the Almighty One. Frequent phrases which were
chanted included "Jah Rastafari!" "Babylon must fall!"
"Sellassie High!"

During refreshments, the daughters of Zion (our
queens) prepared fried fish, curried goat, roast breadfruit
and other delicacies. We churned our own ice-cream
from soursop, coconut (dreadnut), and mixed fruits. The
culture was strongly against the use of alcoholic bever-
ages and pork products. The chalice with weed (incense)

was frequently passed around until the morn. Then all the brethren would depart to their respective ranches happily, delighted, and elated.

On other occasions there were Rastafarian Convention Groundations. These were held only at a reputable camp administered by an elder brethren of eminence. Only then could such a gathering be convened. By invitation, brethren would travel from different parishes and the urban camps to the site of the convention. The agenda listed topics of vital interest to the Rastafarian survival. There were open debates which were often highly opinionated, ardent, furious, and emotional during prolonged sessions. These sessions sometimes lasted for days, yet without personal animosity toward any individual speaker. Although heated at times, an amicable aura would always prevail, even when there was no consensus. Our Rastafarian motto of "Peace and Love" would conclude each debate.

Chapter 8
MY RASTAFARIAN
JOURNEY

Count Ossie

MY RASTAFARIAN JOURNEY

I was born and raised at Windward and Sheffield Roads near Bournemouth Gardens, in the eastern section of Kingston. The surrounding area was a hub of athletic and entertainment activities. There were several sporting clubs nearby which included names such as Wembly, Kensington, Lucas, and the Police Athletic Club. Then there was Doncaster by the sea, nicknamed the "Sahara". Doncaster was the headquarters for the Jamaican Boy Scouts. The local youths took advantage of the swimming pool there for a penny fee. We also frequented the Barnett's Beach, and every now and again we would sneak pass the watchman to get a swim in Sirgany's pool which cost six pence in admission (quite expensive at that time).

Bournemouth Club, managed by the Kingston and Saint Andrew Corporation, was the highlights for swimming, music, dancing, and general entertainment. Dances were held every Wednesday and Friday nights. Some of the great musical bands which performed at Bournemouth from 1940 to the 1960s were Milton McPherson, Redver Cooke, Eric Deans, Roy Coulburn, and Lester Hall. These bands were comprised of musicians such as Wilton "Bra" Gaynair, Sam Walker, Guy Trot, Roland Alphonso, Tommy McCook, "Little G" McNair, Don Drummond, the Hall brothers -Bushie, Lester, and Vivi "One Talent", "Foggy" Mullings, "Trombone" Mullings, Janet Enwright, Cluet "Bassie" Johnson, "Jah" Brevett, "Pappa Son", Clifford "Baba"

Mack, Ralph Aiken, Ernie Rangling, Sonny Bradshaw, Frankie Bonitto, and others. Clifford "Baba" Mack and Ralph Aiken were my father and uncle respectively. The vocalists included Fred Stanley, Julian Iffla, Totlyn Jackson, Carlye Heywood, among others.

Some of these musicians used to rehearse at my home with my father and uncle. The music was primarily American swing and jazz. Knowing these musicians personally, I had great respect and love for their musical talent.

Though the Akete drum was commonly used on the Rastafarian camps, Count Ossie developed a unique style of beat influenced by the talented musicians who often rehearsed at his camp. My elder cousins Derrick "Zorro" and Big David would often take me to Count Ossie's camp to watch some of these rehearsals. On any given night the rehearsal group included Count Ossie's African drums, Big Bra on saxophone, Tommy Mc. on saxophone, Roland Alphonso on saxophone, Don D. on trombone, Carl Masters on trombone, Jah Jerri on guitar, and Vivi Hall on trumpet. At about age twelve (mid 1940's) I went on a journey with my cousin Zorro to Brother Lover's camp in Warieka Hills. It was here that I met Brother Lover for the first time. With his full bearded features, he had a strong resemblance to the Emperor Haile Sellassie I. I was in awe until he greeted me with a warm, "Love youth man". I was dumbfounded. I sat with my cousin and listened to the chanted psalms, some of which I already knew, and I became more at ease.

After we came down from the hills, I asked my cousin why he took me to the Rastafarian camp. He answered, "I took you to let you have your own personal experience and abolish any fears that you might have about Rastafarians." From my experience between Count

Ossie's and Brother Lover's camps I realized that the Rastafarians were a peaceful and religious group of people. I began to reason more with many of them in my neighborhood as I became older. Upon graduation from high school, I went to work at the Daily Gleaner as an assistant to the Editor Mr. T. E. Sealy. Here I developed a passion for journalism. However, after a while I took another job at the Alumina Jamaica Bauxite Plant at Shooters Hill in Manchester. It was during this period that I began to adapt to the tenets of the Rastafarian religious lifestyle. I became very popular on the plant and in the surrounding communities of Shooter's Hill, Content, Williams Field, and Royal Flat area.

In 1959 the workers went on a six weeks strike, a few were unjustly fired, including myself. No explanation was given even though I had done nothing to warrant this. So I returned home on Windward Road where the local youngsters assembled around me. I established a camp in my home with the following brethren around me; Brother Bobby, Big Dike, Brother Les, Brother Monty, Brother Percy, Brother Stanford, Brother Shaggy, Brother Morgie, Brother Sam, Big Brady, Little Bully, Brother Daggo, and Brother Moses.

One night in 1960, at my home on Windward Road, I held a party and gathered together a group of musicians to play. The group included Don Drummond, Brevett, Jah Jerry, Papa Son, Roland Alphonso, and Dizzie Johnny. The party was impromptu but well attended by my surrounding neighbors and brethren. Because of the reception by the audience, I was encouraged to keep this group of musicians together. The group continued to rehearse at my home until Tommy McCook, upon his arrival back to Jamaica, got together with the group to form the famous "Skatalites band." Together they revolutionized Jamaica's music from an Americanized form of jazz and swing to an indigenous Jamaican composition of "Ska". This was the beginning of the original Jamaican dance music. Soon after the Skatalites became world renown for their unique style of music.

In the late 1950's Reverend Claudius Henry, a Jamaican clergyman, returned from the United States and began preaching about the repatriation to Africa. He publicly emphasized that October 31, 1959 was to be the day of restoration. His son Ronald Henry became involved in clandestine activities in the Red Hills Sligoville area. Several shooting incidents occurred and a number of people were killed. Rastafarians were accused of being involved with Ronald Henry. Premier Manley declared a state of emergency and called out the army which subsequently quelled the uprising. Ronald Henry and his American friends were arrested, tried and hung for treason.

Shortly after this period a riot erupted between the Rastafarians and the police along Spanish Town Road. It was then that ninety Rastafarian brethren were arrested. They were defended by counselors Peter Evans and Dudley Thompson. Premier Manley issued a public statement that anywhere Rastafarians were gathered in groups, it should be reported to the police. The brethren, especially those in Kingston, felt threatened. In assessing the situation some brethren advocated armed rebellion in response to the unprovoked attack on Rastafarians.

My brethren and I in eastern and central Kingston were opposed to any armed Rastafarian aggression against the society of Jamaica. I was never anti-social and only wanted an end to British colonial policies in the island. There were heated debates among the brethren about how to settle the volatile situation. Gradually the reasoning of our brethren in eastern and central Kingston prevailed. We agreed to communicate to the government in regards to the situation. It was then that the University of the West Indies dispatched their own team of investigators to assess what had developed.

I then wrote to Premier Manley requesting that he meet with a delegation of Rastafarians from eastern and central Kingston. Premier Manley replied in the affirmative. We met at his office to discuss our concerns. Our delegation included Brother Philmore, Count Ossie, Brother Steretts, Brother Woody, and I (Douglas Mack). We presented a petition of over four thousand signatures electing Brother Philmore Alvaranga and myself as representatives of the brethren of eastern and central Kingston. This meeting culminated in a series of other meetings, which led to Brother Phil and myself being selected on the first official mission to five African countries in 1961.

Chapter 9
FIRST OFFICIAL MISSION TO AFRICA (1961)

In 1960 an investigative report on the Rastafarian movement was compiled by a team of social scientists from the University of the West Indies (U.W.I.). This team consisted of Professor M. J. Smith, Professor Roy Augier, and Rex Nettleford. This report revealed that the Rastafarian brethren had genuine complaints which required the attention of the government. The report stated that the Rastafarian brethren should not be discriminated against in their endeavor to obtain employment, that there should be no discrimination against Rastafarians growing their beard, that the police should not take punitive action against them for assembling on the camps, and that the Jamaican government should contact African governments, particularly Ethiopia, on the brethren's desire to repatriate to Africa.

Premier Norman Manley accepted in principle, the recommendations made by the investigative team from U.W.I. Subsequently he contacted a number of African government, including Ethiopia, about the possibility of repatriating Rastafarian brethren to the continent of Africa. The African government of Ethiopia, Nigeria, Ghana, Liberia, and Sierra-Leone responded that they would welcome a delegation from Jamaica including Rastafarians. Premier Manley then convened a series of meeting with the brethren and other "back to Africa" organizations.

The team selected for the mission was comprised of Brother Philmore Alvaranga, Brother Mortimo Planno and I (Brother Douglas Mack) as representatives of the Rastafarian brethren. Other members of the mission included Mr. Westmore Blackmore of the Universal Negro Improvement Association U.N.I.A.), Dr. M. B. Douglas of the Afro-Caribbean Council, Mr. Z. Monroe-Scarlett of the Afro-West Indian Welfare League, Mr. Cecil G. Gordon of the Ethiopian World Federation Inc., Dr. L. C. Leslie as leader and advisor of the mission, and Mr. Victor Reid as the journalist. The Jamaican delegation was later joined by the Honorable E. H. Lake who was the Minister of Social Welfare in Antigua.

The mission departed from Kingston on April 4th, 1961 by B.O.A.C. aircraft. Our first stop was in New York City. We were met by members of the Ethiopian World Federation, the U.N.I.A., and other back to Africa organizations in New York. Delegates visited and worshiped at the Ethiopian Orthodox Church in Harlem. This was our first physical contact with the Ethiopian church, although we had previous communications with the Ethiopian Orthodox Church in Guyana.

The delegates stayed at the Hotel Theresa (corner of 7th Ave. and 125th St.) in Harlem. This hotel was directly across from a famous book store said to be owned by Elijah Muhammad, where Malcolm X and Muhammad Ali frequented. Hotel Theresa was one of the first black owned hotels in the United States.

We trotted up Lennox Avenue, retracing some of the steps of the Honorable Marcus Garvey during the U.N.I.A. heydays in Harlem. We also visited the famous Cotton Club where entertainment legends like Charlie Yardbird Parker, Miles Davis, Ella Fitzgerald, Billy Holiday, Nat King Cole, Ruth Brown, and Billy Eckstine performed.

Our main reason for visiting New York was to obtain visas from the Liberian Consulate. One must remember that during that time we were still classified as British subjects.

On Thursday, April 6th, the mission departed from New York by Pan American Airways for London. We arrived in London Friday April 7th. We stayed at the Hotel Londoner on Welbeck Street. Our mission was met by a large group of West Indian immigrants residing in England. Like New York, our stay in London was primarily to obtain entry visas to Sudan, Ghana, Nigeria, and Sierra-Leone. These African countries, with the exception of Ghana (1957), had recently obtained their independence from Great Britain.

While in London, the mission visited many places of interest including the British House of Parliament, West Minister Abbey, Madam Toussard's Wax Museum, Hyde Park, Piccadilly, and Buckingham Palace where we observed the changing of the guards. I visited a brother called Judgment at his home in Kensington where I had a reunion with one of my cousins Derrick "Zorro".

Zorro left Jamaica in 1940 and enlisted in the Royal Airforce. He returned to Jamaica after the war, but left for England again in the late 1950's. So I had not seen him for quite some time but he was one of my favorite relatives. We reminisced about our experience on brother Lover's camp. He gave me a large King James Authorized Version of the Bible with the books of the Apocrypha. Before this I had only heard of stories about the Macabees, but had never read about it. So the first thing I did was turn the pages of the Apocrypha to read about Judas Macabeus. This Bible still remains in-tact in my possession to this day.

The mission departed from London for Khartoum, Sudan via Rome on April 14th. We made a brief stop in Rome and arrived in Khartoum on April 15th. Our delegation stayed at the Grand Hotel on the banks of the fabled River Nile. This was our first landing on African soil.

After checking in at the hotel, Brothers Planno, Phil, and I walked across the street to the banks of the river, where we took off our shoes and bathed our tired feet in the cool water of the Nile. We reminisced about the prophet Moses as a babe drifting down the Nile in a basket of bulrushes. All around us was the black stoic faces of the Sudanese Moslems. Moses the prophet had to be a black African, we deduced. This was the authentic Moses cradle, the bulrushes, and the river Nile. What hypocrisy we bellowed! Europe's religious preachers teaching us about a white Moses and a white Jesus. Indeed Europe's artists missed their mark and made Christ's portrait look not dark!

The Sudan bordered Ethiopian northern provinces. The Blue Abbai (Blue Nile) flows from Ethiopia converging with the White Nile at the cataract in Khartoum, then flows on to Egypt and the Mediterranean Sea. The Nile is 4,400 miles of magnificent serpentine continuous flow. That mighty river watered the Garden of Eden (Genesis, Chapter 2).

Our delegation drove by motorcade from Khartoum to the town of Omdurman where we visited the ancient house of Caliph. The Caliph led his Sudanese tribesmen (the Derwishers) to victory over the British forces led by General Gordon and General Kitchener. General Gordon was slain in this battle and General Kitchener was held captive. We left Sudan for Ethiopia on the Ethiopian Airlines.

ETHIOPIA

As the aircraft captain announced in English, "We are now crossing the Ethiopian frontier," we were met by a squadron of Ethiopian fighter jets. The captain informed us that we were being escorted by the Ethiopian airforce to the airport in Asmara. Our delegation roared as we watched the aerobatics maneuvers of the Ethiopian fighter jets, which were displaying this performance to welcome us. The mission landed in Asmara by the Red Sea but we did not disembark. A group of Ethiopian priests boarded the plane to accompany us on our journey to Addis Ababa.

We arrived in Addis Ababa April 16th. Ethiopia was the mission's first official destination. Upon arrival in Addis Ababa we were met and greeted by a deputation of government officials. Among them were Ato Getaneh Haile Mariam, Lidj Ayele-Worq Abebe from the Ministry of Foreign Affairs, and Woizaro Maize from the Ministry of Education. Lidj Ayele-Worq Abebe was assigned as the liaison officer and escort for our entire tour of Ethiopia. We stayed at the Hotel Ghion.

Later that day our delegates visited His Holiness the Abuna Basilios, Archbishop and Patriarch of the Ethiopian Orthodox Church at his official residence the Patriarchate. The Rastafarian delegates discussed the divinity of H.I.M. Emperor Haile Sellassie as the return Messiah from the royal house of King David. The brethren recited many biblical verses from the book of Revelations and Acts of the Apostles. We also discussed the dynasty of His Imperial Majesty's ancestry, traced to Cush 6,500 B.C. and to Ori 10,000 B.C. We also discussed the successive Italian invasion of Ethiopia and His Imperial Majesty's prophesies to the League of Nations when he told them that God and history will remember their judgment if they did not bow before the accomplished facts. We reminisced about the Emperor telling the League of Nations, "You have struck the match in Ethiopia but it shall burn Europe." We reminded the Archbishop of Revelation, Chapter 17 -verse 14, " These shall make war with the lamb, and the lamb shall overcome them: for He is Lord of Lords and King of Kings." At the conclusion of our discussion Abuna Basillios said that the Bible could be interpreted that way.

During our discussion the delegates were served tea and "Tej" (honey wine). The brethren were vindicated by His Holiness acknowledgment. The Patriarch then gave each member of the delegation an Ethiopian robe. He then told us that he did not give us the robes just for gifts, but that we should know ourselves to be Ethiopians. I was later informed that the insignia on my robe signified the title "Dejatchmatch," meaning rear guard general. We left his presence rejoicing.

While our delegates awaited His Majesty's audience, Mr. Abebe guided us through our itinerary. We held discussions with the Minister of Foreign Affairs, the Minister of the Interior, the Minister of Commerce and Industry, the Minister of Agriculture, and the Minister of National Community Development. Our mission was warmly received by each minister as we delved into discussions of repatriation to our motherland. The ministers agreed that various avenues of such an endeavor would be further investigated by the government.

Next we visited Sheshamane about 200 kilometers from Addis Ababa. This was the land granted to the people of African descent in the western hemisphere in gratitude for their assistance to Ethiopia during the war with Italy. (1935-1941).

Residing on the land were James and Helen Piper, a couple originally from Monsterrat in the Caribbean. The Pipers migrated from Monsterrat to New York and joined the Ethiopian World federation. They later migrated to Ethiopia in 1948 with a group of other West Indians including Julia Green from Anotto Bay in Jamaica, and Dr. David Talbot from British Guyana. They settled in Sheshamane, built a small community, and operated a farm where they grew sunflower, corn, bananas, and other crops. They also had a herd of goats and about fifty cows.

The Pipers also owned and ran a small corn mill. They grounded corn for the surrounding tribes for a nominal fee. At the time of our visit only the Pipers remained at Sheshamane. Dr. Talbot was now working for the Ethiopian Ministry of Information and lived in Addis Ababa, where we met him.

In Sheshamane our mission delegates sampled the Ethiopian national dish of Enjera and Wat. Enjera is a flat, soft, uneven bread baked from sour dough, made from a wheat-like plant called Tef. Wat is a sauce with meat highly spiced with onions, peppers, etc.; not a dish recommended for a nervous stomach though very tasty.

On Friday April 21st the mission was granted an audience with His Imperial Majesty at the Imperial Palace in Addis Ababa. We were introduced by Ato Tafara Kidane Worq Wold. Dr. Leslie outlined our delegation's purpose for the visit to investigate the possibility of resettling in Ethiopia people of African descent from Jamaica and other Caribbean islands. Emperor Haile Sellassie was a man of small stature, dressed in decorative military attire, with a warm pleasant disposition and impeccable mannerism. His Imperial Majesty replied in Amharic which was interpreted to us by Ato Tafara Worq. The

Emperor said that he knew the black people of the west, particularly Jamaica, were blood brothers to the Ethiopians. He also knew that slaves were sent to Jamaica from Ethiopia. Continuing, the Emperor said that Ethiopia was large enough to accommodate all the people of African descent living in the Caribbean with the desire to return. He told us that Ethiopia would always be open to those who wanted to return home. His Imperial Majesty expressed the desire for an exchange of scholars between Ethiopia and countries of the West Indians.

In regard to resettlement the Emperor said that a panel of experts would be selected to discuss the various details of such a migration. He said that he hoped we would send the right people. The Emperor then gave a gold medal to each member of the delegation. Our delegation thanked His Imperial Majesty and issued him an invitation to visit Jamaica in the near future. He quickly accepted promising to visit soon.

Other members of the delegations departed except the Rastafarian brothers Planno, Alvaranga, and I. We had brought special gifts to present to Him and had the desire to speak with Him personally. Brother Phil presented a wooden map of Africa carved from mahogany, cedar, and mahoe. The plague displayed a carved portrait of His Imperial Majesty on one side of the wooden case. The Emperor smiled and spoke in English for the first time, "That's Africa...is it from the Rastafari brethren?" We all replied in unison, "Yes Your Majesty." We told him that the carver was a Rastafarian brethren named Bal Boa, who was also the maker of our Akete drums.

I presented photographs of many places in Jamaica and many Rastafarian brethren, and also a painting of

Navy Island. His Imperial Majesty said, "Photographs of the brethren?" "Thank You."

Brother Planno presented a woven scarf in red, gold, and green (the colors of the Ethiopian flag). The Emperor Haile Sellassie asked, "Was this woven by you?" Brother Planno answered, "Yes Your Majesty." Smiling the Emperor said, "Thank you." We bowed and departed from the Imperial Court. We likened this visit to the three wise men (the Magi) paying homage and bearing gifts to the King of Kings.

The next day we traveled by plane to the Awash Valley. It was indicated to us that in addition to Sheshamane, this was a prospective area for resettlement. The valley was surrounded by rolling hills, green and fertile, with a river running through it. On April 23rd our mission departed from Addis Ababa, by Ethiopian Airlines, for Nigeria.

NIGERIA

We arrived in Lagos, Nigeria after twelve hours of flight. The delegation was met by Nigerian government officials led by Mr. Babatunde Harper of the Ministry of Internal Affairs. Our delegation stayed at the Federal Palace Hotel in Lagos. Our first visit was to the Oba Adele (the king of Lagos). In greeting us the Oba said that West Indians coming to Africa would be returning to the land of their fathers. He hosted a party for the delegation.

Next we sat through a series of meetings, the first of which included the Minister of Labor and Social Welfare-the Honorable A. J. Johnstone. Mr. Johnstone was of West Indian heritage. We then met with the minister of state-

Dr. Esin Esin. One of our highlights involved an official meeting with the governor general of Nigeria-Dr. Nnamdi Azikiwi (Dr. Zik) at State House, his official residence. A reception was held there in honor of our delegation. Dr. Leslie explained the purpose of our visit to the governor general. Dr. Zik, as he was popularly called, welcomed the mission and said that he was inspired by the philosophies of Marcus Garvey, and that he was educated by West Indian teachers. The governor general lauded the West Indian teachers, pastors, tradesmen, etc. who settled in his country. He said that Nigeria owed a debt to these people, who helped a great deal to establish the independence of Nigeria.

Dr. Zik also said that he hoped that further talks on resettlement would follow, and the question of migration be taken up at official government levels. Dr. Esin Esin was present and also welcomed the mission. He remarked that the people of the West Indies at this point in time, were more socially advanced than the Africans, and that could create problems. But the government of Africa and the West Indies could work to address those problems.

Dr. Esin compared the "Back to Africa Movement" with the Jewish restoration of Israel. He said that Nigeria could absorb all the people of the West Indies who wanted to return home without any problem. In conclusion, he said that the people of African origin in the west were bound to come home.

Our mission visited all the regions that comprised the federation of Nigeria at that time. They were the western, eastern, and northern regions. We visited the capital city of Ibadan in western Nigeria. There we met many West Indian residents. Among them was Mr. D. A. R. Alexander, the solicitor general of western Nigeria. Mr.

Alexander was from Saint Lucia and his wife was from Jamaica.

Next we traveled by airplane to the northern region. We disembarked at kaduna, the capital. Our delegation had hoped to meet with the premier-Sir Ahmadu Bello, the Sardauna of Sokoto, but he was away on business. We visited the walled city of Zaria, about sixty miles from Kaduna. The people of the northern region were mostly devoted Moslems. The area around Zaria was mostly hot, humid, and desertlike-much to our dislike. However, the natives were very friendly. We met several students from the law school and various vendors from the market place. They made beautiful carvings from wood and brass which they sold to visitors and the dishes were similar to those which were familiar to us. Their diet included peas, beans, lamb, watermelon, mangoes, oranges, and an abundance of peanuts (called groundnuts).

After three days we departed for a visit to the eastern region. On Thursday, May 4th, the mission was flown by Nigerian Airways to Enugu, capital of the eastern region. We met with the governor -Sir Francis Ibiam and the premier-Dr. Michael Okpara. Dr. Okpara held a dinner in our honor at the premier's lodge. Our mission members outlined the purpose of our visit. Dr. Okpara welcomed the mission and referred to the delegates as his African brothers. He said that he was very pleased to see us all now look to Africa as our home. For Africa is the original home of all black people. Dr. Okpara apologized to the delegation for his ancestors of the Ibo tribe who use to sell their brothers in slavery to America, the West Indies, and other parts of the world. He was glad to see that all was forgiven.

Premier Okpara said that the Ibo tribe had a law stating that anyone who was able to trace his descent back to this tribe would be immediately received into it; they would bring you back to Ibo land from any part of the world, and your land according to parent's possession, would be restored to you. The premier further stated that Africans, wherever they were living, were welcome in a free Nigeria, and Nigeria had land to accommodate them. In conclusion, the premier said, "Africa welcomes us all, both skilled and unskilled, and my government will follow up this question of repatriation."

Our next meeting was with the provincial publicity manager of the eastern region-Mr. K. O. K. Onyioha. He told the mission members that he had sent a letter to the government of Jamaica, offering lands from the Nkporo clan in Bende, to any Jamaican of African descent whose desire was to return. We fell in love with Enugu because the surroundings looked as familiar as our own Jamaica and the people were as warm-spirited as our own. Enugu was landscaped with many hills with a climate similar to that of Mandeville's in Jamaica. We eventually left Enugu and flew to Lagos for an overnight stay. The next day we boarded the Nigerian Airways for Ghana.

GHANA "THE GOLD COAST"

On Monday May 8th, our mission arrived in Accra, the capital of the republic of Ghana. We checked into the Ambassador Hotel where a reception was held the next day in our honor. We met with the house of chiefs from the various states in Ghana. Among them was the Nii Amoo Nakwah II, the Obtobulum Mensah (paramount chief of all chiefs). He was ninety-two years of age and in

Nii Amo Nakwah II, the Obtobulum Mensah,
Paramount Chief of the Ashanti praying for members of
the Jamaican Back to Africa Delegation, in Accra Ghana
1961.(In center of picture, with dark jacket is the author
Brother Douglas Mack).

the best of health. Nii Amoo informed us that he remembered and knew of past times when slaves were leaving Ghana, and that agreements were made between the Portuguese, the Dutch, and the Ghananian chiefs to return these slaves after a given period of time. But they never returned.

He said that seeing us reminded him of some of those people; and the time had come for our return. The chief prayed and blessed us in his Ashanti language.

During this visit we met two brothers living in Accra who were our associates from Jamaica. One was Brother Jackie Payne, a compositor and printer. He was a close friend of mine from his working days at the Daily Gleaner on Harbour Street in the 1950's.

On Wednesday, May 10th, the mission met the Osagefo, Dr. Kwame Nkrumah. He was the president of the Republic of Ghana, and Ghana was the first country in Africa to gain independence from England in 1957. At Flag Staff House in Accra, where Dr. Nkrumah resided, our delegation was greeted with a warm welcome. Dr. Nkrumah told us that our meeting was an historical one, not only because we were blood brothers, but because so many attempts were made and had failed to bring Africans from the west back home to the continent of Africa. He reminisced how Marcus Garvey had tried and was sabotaged; but our mission could not be sabotaged because this was the opportune moment for negotiating resettlement. He went on to say that Ghana had an area of over 100,000 square miles, which meant that they had sufficient space to accommodate people. "Look upon yourselves as Africans and land is here for the asking," he said.

This wise president of Ghana expressed his agreement with the "Back to Africa Movement" and he paid tribute to Marcus Garvey, who had been his inspiration. He told us that the Africans in the West Indies and the Africans in Africa had developed separately over the intervening years, and that there would be problems of adjusting to be overcome. The Osagefo went on to say that the Black Star Line fleet would be at our disposal when we were ready to make our transition. He applauded many of his teachers, who were Jamaicans, and asked to be remembered by Dr. Ivan Lloyd. He also asked our delegation for a bust and some pictures of Marcus Garvey. Dr. Leslie, our mission leader, assured him that as soon as we returned to Jamaica his wishes would be granted.

Dr. Nkrumah appointed a special committee to discuss the situation with us. Our mission met with the special committee on Thursday, May 11th. The committee members included the following:

1) Dei Anang from the Ministry of Foreign Affairs
2) Sir Tisbo Darku who was the chairman of the Cocoa Marketing Board
3) Enoch Okoh who was the principal secretary to the president
4) Dr. Nana Kobina Nkersia IV who was paramount chief of Essi Kadu and Ambassador Plenipotentiary
5) Tawia Adamafio who was the Minister for Presidential Affairs.

The committee inquired about the number of people who desired to return and the type of skills available. I pointed out to the committee that we had no accurate number available at that moment; but that I expected it to be in the thousands. Addressing the committee I replied, "I am a machinist and pipe fitter, Brother Philmore is a shoemaker and farmer, Brother Planno is a weaver, Mr. Blackwood (from the UNIA) is a potter, Mr. Gordon (from the Ethiopian World Federation) is a port worker, Mr. Z. Monroe Scarlett (from the Afro West Indian Welfare League) is a chiropractor, Dr. Douglas "Danquah" (from the Afro Caribbean League) is a dental surgeon, Dr. Leslie (our leader) is a surgeon internist, and Mr. Victor Reid is a journalist." We also informed the committee that most Jamaicans were capable farmers. On a final note the committee stated that follow-ups were needed by the government of Ghana and Jamaica.

LIBERIA

Our mission left Ghana and arrived by Pan American Airways at Robertsfield Airport in Liberia on May 16th. We drove to Monrovia, about fifty miles from the airport. We drove through miles of rubber tree plantations owned by the Firestone Company. Our delegation stayed at the Ducor Palace Hotel in Monrovia. The country Liberia was founded by about eighty-eight members of the "Back to Africa Movement" who migrated from New York. They bought land from the tribal chiefs and settled on it.

On Thursday, May 18th, the mission met with President Tubman at the Presidential Offices in Monrovia. Our delegation was warmly greeted by the president who informed us that ever since the Republic of Liberia was founded, immigration laws were enacted to allow for people of African descent from the West Indies and elsewhere to settle in the country. Furthermore, in 1955 a provision was made to issue free land to immigrants and

Members of the Jamaician Back to Africa delegation with President Dr. Kwame Nkrumah, Accra Ghana, 1961.

Standing left to right, Munroe Scarlett, Mr. Victor Reid, Dr. Leslie, President Nkrumah, Brother Douglas Mack, Brother Mortimo Planno, Honorable E.H. Lake Minister of Social Welfare Antiqua, Brother Philmore Alvaranga, and Ghanian Protocol Chief.

(Sitting left to right Mr. Blackwood, the U.N.I.A. Delegate and Mr. Gordon representing the Ethiopian World Federation).

The president spoke highly of the Honorable Marcus Garvey and said that he adored his work. He also stated that many West Indians had made great contributions to the Liberian society. The president held a dinner for us on Friday, May 19th, at the Coo Coo's Nest, a countryside restaurant. He asked the Rastafarian brethren to bless the table before the meals were served. Brothers Philmore, Planno, and I responded with the prayer, "Princes shall come out of Egypt; Ethiopia shall stretch forth her hands unto God. Thy blessings that the hungry be fed; the naked clothed; the sick nourished; the aged protected; and the infants cared for through the grace of Jah. Selah."

During the course of the dinner the president asked us to inform him of the Rastafarian Movement, which we did. After defining spiritual conceptions concerning His Imperial Majesty Emperor Haile Selassie I, President Tubman said that Liberia was open to all people of African descent, whether they were Rastafari or not. He reminded us of his visit to Jamaica; and said that Jamaica was over populated while Liberia was under populated and needed people. He stated that all immigrants wishing to settle in Liberia would be required to have a clean police record.

Liberia was already producing banana, rice, coffee, palm oil, and rubber. It had mines of gold, diamond, lead, and graphite; but Liberia did not produce any sugar. Many West Indians were expert farmers of sugarcane and knew how to produce sugar.

Our mission departed on Sunday, May 21st for Sierra Leone.

SIERRA LEONE

On Sunday, May 21st, after two hours of flight, we arrived in Sierra Leone. We traveled from the airport by ferry boat to Freetown. Sierra Leone was our final official call, although we would later stop in Dakar, Senegal before our return to Jamaica.

Sierra Leone had just received independence about one month earlier—April 27th to be exact. They were still celebrating their freedom.

Monday, May 22nd was the day we met with Dr. Sir Milton Margai, the Prime Minister of Sierra Leone. He welcomed us and told us that Sierra Leone was founded for the former slaves emancipated in Britain, America, and the West Indies. He went on to say that in 1778 over 200 black people were brought back from the west to help to build the capital city called Freetown. The Prime Minister accepted the principles of repatriation of African descendants from the west. He said that Sierra Leone could use the skills of our people.

However, having just gained independence, Sir Milton said Sierra Leone needed a time to settle down; but his government would consider the proposition at a later date.

Sierra Leone was a beautiful country of about 28,000 square miles. They mined diamonds, bauxite, and iron ore. Our mission visited the Marampa Iron Ore Mines.

On Tuesday, May 30th, the mission departed from Sierra Leone for Dakar Senegal where we made our connecting flight to Lisbon, Portugal. We spent three days in Lisbon before departing by Avianca Aircraft for San Juan, Puerto Rico. We made a brief stop to refuel in Santa Maria. It was an all night flight across the Atlantic Ocean

to get to San Juan; but we got there on June 3rd at about
7:30 a.m. We made a 12:30 p.m. connecting flight from
San Juan to Kingston, Jamaica by BWIA.

Our plane touched down in Kingston at approximately 2:45 p.m. to a tremendous welcome by a tumultuous body of brethren at the Palisados Airport (now
called the Norman Washington Manley Airport). Upon
arrival the Rastafarian delegates, followed by a large
crowd, gave a public address at Race Course (now called
National Heroes Park). Soon after our arrival, the
Rastafarian members of the mission compiled a report
and summary of the tour and gave it to the Parliament of
Jamaica for their deliberations. This report was signed by
Philmore Alvaranga, Mortimo Planno, and I (Douglas
Mack). The other members of the mission also prepared
a separate report which they presented to Premier
Manley's officials.

One early dawn about two months after our arrival
back to Jamaica, a large contingent of police, led by
Detective Ted Ansel, swooped on my camp in the
Warieka Hills. They held us at gunpoint while they
burned our dwellings and all our earthly possessions. All
the maps, books, and literature I gathered on my African
tour went up in flames. We protested vigorously, but I
was threatened to be shot. No one was arrested for any
wrong doing, yet we were never compensated for the
loss. The only thing that I managed to salvage was the
Bible given to me by my cousin Zorro in London.
Babylon continued to wage war with the lamb!

LETTER TO HON. N.W. MANLEY, Q.C.

Hon. N.W. Manley, Q.C.
Premier
Ministry of Development

Dear Sir:

Greetings in perfect love from we the Rastafarian members of the Back-to Africa mission, recently returned to the island.

As you may have already heard, Sir, we have refused to attach our signatures to a report drafted by Mr. Reid, co-adviser to the delegation.

Our reason for not signing Hon. Premier, is that we thought all the delegates would assemble for two weeks, (as was expressed by you before the mission's departure) Sir, and compile a report with each delegate's experience of the tour, in it.

Instead of a joint draft by us all, the draft was prepared by Mr. Reid and submitted to the delegates for correction and study.

The study of Mr. Reid's working draft was done under the most dictatorial terms. The draft was so termed, that we disagreed with almost every statement used. The terms minimize the gravity of the facts gathered by the mission during the African tour.

The mission to Africa was stated to be a fact-finding one, sponsored by your Government, Hon. Sir, and with the presentation of the facts, any lack of understanding that may exist among the people of Jamaica, including Rastafarians, should be eliminated by the publishing of such facts.

It is not history—the undisputable facts of slave-trading, the children of our forefathers were forcibly and brutally torn from their mothers' bosom, and from our ancestral home Africa and brought to the colonial plantations in the West for the sole purpose of filling the colonial coffers of Europe.

The right of this wrong, can only be achieved by the eventual repatriation of all captured souls, who so desire, Hon. Premier.

This was the way in which we presented our cause of repatriation to the African Governments. The desirous people of African descent, who have chosen Africa as their place of rest, should not be retarded or made to feel frustrated in their desire.

Emperor Haile Sellassie I has said "to send the right people" and he knows that the black people of the West an particularly Jamaica are blood brothers to the Ethiopians.

The Abuna also said (to the entire mission with the exception of Mr. Reid) that we should all know ourselves to be Ethiopians.

We the Rastafarian brethern claim Ethiopian ancestry in Jamaica years ago and it is principally through us that a mission was sent to Africa: that is why we should all have sat together and compile a report instead of being asked to correct one which was completely short of facts, Sir.

Furthermore, President Tubman's speech was omitted from Mr. Reid's report.

The President stated that liberia welcomes all people of African descent, whether they say Rastafari is God or not.

Although the mission sat for approximately eight

hours correcting the draft prepared by Mr. Reid, the final draft is still short of facts, and there are statements in it which have yet to be omitted, Sir.

Under such circumstances, we have written our own report, which contains facts which we can verify.

We also ask that the Agenda presented to you by Mack and Alvaragna (at our first meeting in November last year) be given due consideration and approval by you Sir, as we are at present using every measure of our love to unite the brethren for a better understanding towards Government and the public in general.

"Our peace we leave with Thee, not at this world giveth Thee."

Sincerely yours,
Philmore Alvaranga
Douglas Mack
Mortimo Planno

Rastafarian Delegates,
Back-to-Africa Mission

Chapter 10
Second Mission to Africa (1963-1965)

A ccording to the 1961 mission dialogue with the government to Ghana, Ethiopia, Liberia, Nigeria, and Sierra Leone, further negotiations and consultations were to be arranged between these African countries and the government of Jamaica. Contacts were to be made by emissaries of all these governments, to create an outline for immigrant settlement in these African countries. I sent correspondence to Premier Manley and the African governments entreating them to exploit the situation with some haste.

At this point in time Jamaica was a partner in a West Indian federation with Trinidad and Tobago, Barbados, Leeward and Windward islands, Grenada, Saint Lucia, and Saint Vincent. Then in 1962 Jamaica seceded and formed a new government under the premiership of the Honorable William Alexander Bustamante.

For over two years despite our repeated request to explore the avenues for repatriation, our government did nothing to enhance the situation. Things appeared to be quite dismal. Inevitably, disturbances arose. Trouble developed in the Coral Gardens area of Montego Bay between a group of Rastafarian brethren and some civilians on Holy Thursday, April 11th,1963. There were casualties; and Premier Bustamante himself led the defense force operation to quell the disturbance. Many brethren were beaten, killed, and arrested.

Brother Philmore and I decided to go to the Montego Bay area to assess the situation for ourselves. The news media was actually declaring war islandwide on Rastafarians for the outbreak. We promptly requested a meeting with Premier Bustamante in order to discuss what had developed. Premier Bustamante agreed to meet with us at his east Race Course office. The delegation comprised of Brother Count Ossie, Brother Philmore, Brother Moses, and myself attended the meeting.

We discussed the current situation of violence, and accused the police of over reacting and using excessive force to the point of genocide, because many brethren were being harassed and killed. The Commissioner of Police, Mr. H. Gordon Langdon who was present at the meeting, accused us of declaring war on the society. We denied the allegations. I pointed out the fact that over the years our brethren, though vociferous advocates of a particular culture, had always remained passive and nonviolent in their respective communities. To this premier Bustamante agreed. I went on to say that Brother Philmore and I were embarking on a tour of the Montego Bay area to ascertain the facts of the situation, as opposed to the media's reports. Mr. Bustamante advised us not to go because he could not guarantee our safety in that area.

I responded to Premier Bustamante telling him that it would be a sorry day if the elected government could not guarantee the safety of its citizens on the public thoroughfare. After all the safety and well being of its citizens were the government s prime and foremost responsibility. Mr. Bustamante concurred; and we told him and the commissioner that we would be going to Montego Bay the next day. We then asked him to sponsor another mission to Africa to further the negotiations already set forth by the previous government. Premier Bustamante refused and said he would not spend one penny on such a venture. At this point we made the argument that we would sponsor a second mission to Africa ourselves; and asked if his government would block or object to this plan. He assured us that his government would not interfere with such a mission; then he gave us his blessings.

Our tour of Montego Bay included the areas of Mount Salem, Glendevon, and Coral Gardens. This tour revealed that many brethren were being suppressed arbitrarily by the police. Consequently we dispatched letters to Premier Bustamante, the respective government's of Africa, and to the United Nations, accusing the government of Jamaica of genocidal actions, and insisting that these actions be stopped.

Since the government refused to sponsor our second mission to Africa, Brother Phil and I campaigned to raise the necessary funds. We first consulted Mr. Reid -Justice of the Peace and owner of the club Adastra Gardens. He was very enthused and was instrumental in the effort of raising funds for the mission. He gave us our first donation and signed a letter recommending us to a number of prominent business associates. Among them were Mr. Billings -owner of Billings Bedding Company on Spanish Town Road and Mr. MacGregor -a fruit exporter, also located on Spanish Town Road. Mr. Louis Chen -a prominent businessman in the Rockford area, was also a dedicated contributor to the cause. We then kept a series of dances throughout the corporate area to foster additional funds. The dance sites included Tiverton Road, Liberty Hall, Forrester's Hall, The Gold Coast Club, Copa Cobana, and Montego Bay. These dance sessions were well attended. The musical selections were by Duke Reid, Coxson's Downbeat, and The Matador. Special attractions at midnight were provided by Count Ossie and his African drums, along with Don Drummond, Dizzy Johnnie, Little Bra Gaynair, Jah Jerry, and Jah Brevett. No doubt the fund raising effort was a great success.

On December 22nd, 1963, Brother Philmore and I departed for New York on the first stop of our second mission to Africa. We carried with us a petition of over three thousand signatures in support of our genocidal grievance against the government of Jamaica. We took along a wooden carving of the continent of Africa, depicting Africa's influence on the world. This was the gift we brought for His Imperial Majesty Emperor Haile Sellassie I. We also had in our possession a special wooden carving of Africa, balancing the scales of justice to be presented to the United Nations Organization. The map was made to highlight the prophecy "Mene mene tekel upharsin peres," meaning -Africa balanced the nations of the world and found them wanting.

In New York we were met by members of the U.N.I.A., the Ethiopian World Federation, and others. We immediately attended a service at the Ethiopian Orthodox Church in Harlem. After the service, we were asked to address an audience regarding our mission. In my address I pointed out that this was a follow-up of the first "Back to Africa" mission of 1961. I explained that we were enroute to Addis Ababa to once again meet with His Imperial Majesty in the hope of addressing a session of the newly formed Organization of African Unity. This organization was currently meeting in Cairo, Egypt. I went on to say that we were in possession of a petition to the United Nations Organization, seeking assistance for reparations for the slave trade, to be used in the settlement of the brethren on the African continent. We asked the Ethiopian Orthodox Church members to grant us accommodations for our sojourn in the United States.

Brother Gladstone Robinson (a member of the Ethiopian World Federation), volunteered to accommodate us during our stay in the U.S.A. After the meeting, Brother Robinson drove us to his home in Brooklyn where he provided us with an apartment. This was our first Christmas away from home; and for the first time-we experienced a snow storm.

In the first week of January 1964, we were joined by Brother Samuel Clayton who came in from Kingston. Together we visited the office of the United Nations Organization hoping to meet with Dr. UThant, the Secretary General of the organization. We were informed that Mr. UThant was away in Cairo at the O.A.S. session. Instead, we met with Dr. Mushen Lynn and Dr. Pedro Yap. They were under-secretaries to Dr. UThant. Our delegation gave the under-secretaries the wooden map and our petition asking the U.N.O. to assist the Rastafarian brethren in stopping the Jamaican government from its discriminatory practices and genocidal acts against the Rastafarians. The petition also asked the former slave trading countries such as Great Britain, France, Spain, Portugal, Italy, Belgium, and Holland for reparations and assistance in resettling people of African descent from the western hemisphere, who had the desire to return to their own vine and fig tree.

Dr. Mushen Lynn, in response to our petition, said that the U.N.O. could not act on the presentation of any individual or organization; but if any member government tabled a request on these circumstances, the U.N.O. would be empowered to investigate. Continuing Dr. Lynn said that our mission should therefore try to get any African government to make such a request. We informed Dr. Lynn, that was exactly what our mission was pursuing.

During our sojourn in the United States, from December 1963 to April 1964, our delegation made requests to various African embassies to sponsor our present mission to their respective countries, in the effort of continuing the dialogue of the 1961 mission. The embassies we contacted were Ethiopia, Liberia, Ghana, and Nigeria.

Brother Robinson drove us from New York to Washington D.C. so that we could meet with these African ambassadors. Although we met with them, we could not get any commitment from them to sponsor our mission. Eventually, we decided to activate our own sponsorship, as we did in Jamaica. Consequently we frequently toured the Jamaican communities, especially in Brooklyn where many brethren of Rastafarian persuasion that we knew very well lived.

With Brother Robinson's sterling assistance, we gathered for weekly meetings at his home in Brooklyn. These meetings were well attended; and out of this came the formation of an organization, which we called the (A.R.C.) African Repatriation Committee. Brother Robinson was nominated as the chairman, Brother Daggo was the general secretary, and Sister Roslyn was the honorable treasurer. Brother Phil, Sam, and myself were nominated as ambassador plenipotentiaries. Other founding members included Brother Mario, Brother Chilly, Brother Sleazy, Brother Diaz, Brother Neville, Brother Percy, and Sister Bobby G.

The A.R.C. members became closely associated with another group of Afro-Americans known as The House of Judah. The House of Judah also nominated us as their ambassadors. During our meetings we asked for special donations towards sponsoring our passages to Africa.

Second Mission Members 1963 with left Gladstone
Robinson (International President of the Ethiopian
World's Federation) and Ato Ayele-Worq Abebe.
Ethiopian Consul, at the Ethiopian Consulate N.Y. 1964.

We also held a series of dances to raise funds for the mission. We eventually accrued the finances and then booked our passages to Lagos, Nigeria.

Before our delegation left New York, we met the world heavy weight boxing champion, Muhammad Ali. We exchanged gifts. He gave me his autograph and I presented him with an autographed copy of the J. A. Rogers' book entitled "100 Amazing Facts About The Negro. " The champ and I discussed the possibility of a meeting with Malcolm X, which never materialized because of Brother Malcolm's assassination. With our organization "The A.R.C." in full swing, the mission departed for Lagos, Nigeria on April 29th, 1964.

NIGERIA

Upon our arrival in Lagos, Nigeria, we were met by several officials from the Ministry of Foreign Affairs. Among them were Mr. Babatunde Harper and Mr. Adeoye. We asked the federal government of Nigeria to:

a) Meet with our delegation to continue talks on the settlement proposition of 1961

b) Make the necessary arrangements to send our mission to Addis Ababa after our visit in Nigeria.

c) Provide accommodations for our mission members during our stay in Nigeria.

We were given accommodations for two weeks, during which time we were denied meetings with any minister of government. At the end of the two week period, Mr. Adeoye paid us a visit to inform us that his government had decided to terminate the accommodations and to give us return passages to Kingston, Jamaica. We refused to accept that proposition and told him to report back to his superiors that we would be staying with Mr.

Akintola Moss at Apapa Road, in Ebute Metta. Mr. Moss was a Nigerian, born of Jamaican father. His family returned to Jamaica when Akintola was a young boy. I went to school with him and his brothers Oladipo and Cedric. I became close friends with the family. Akintola returned to reside in Nigeria in the late 1950s, leaving his brothers and sister behind in Jamaica.

We were re-united with Brother Lionel "Jackie" Payne, a school friend of mine, who was now residing in Nigeria. Brother Akin was an accomplished pianist who frequently entertained us at nights. We often backed up his musical expressions with the beating of our Akete drums. We became associated with a Nigerian brother named Ulu. He became our guide around the city; as we toured the market areas and the beach. We saw many fishermen pulling their nets, children bathing in the ocean, and a huge skeleton of a whale about thirty feet in length. We ate lots of roast fish, fufu, gari, mangoes, plantains, and peanuts. Gari was made from pounded cassava and fufu from pounded yams. There were mountains of peanuts (called groundnuts). They were stacked in large mounds for exports; some as high as twenty feet. I had never seen so much peanuts before in my life. Nigeria also produces plenty of palm and coconut oil.

At the marketplace in Ebute Metta, I saw tribesmen with live snakes around their necks, hands, and other parts of their bodies. One man in particular, had a boaconstrictor around his neck, another around his waist, and another around his hand. This startled me a lot because I had never before seen that kind of intimacy between man and reptile. These tribesmen seem quite comfortable with their animals. I took comfort in the scriptural thought that "Man has dominion over the beasts and reptiles; the fowls of the air; and the fish of the sea."

While we were in Lagos, Muhammad Ali was also there on tour. We met him again and renewed our acquaintance. When he inquired and discovered that we were without sponsorship, he extended his generosity and donated some cash to our welfare.

Dr. Michael Okpara, the premier of Eastern Nigeria, flew to Lagos for a meeting with the federal government. Our delegation greeted him upon his arrival. When he saw us he said, "These are my Jamaican friends." He then invited us to join his entourage. We explained to him the nature of our mission and the refusal of the Nigerian government to assist us. Dr. Okpara promised to discuss the matter when he met with the federal prime minister, Sir Abu Bakar Tafewa Balewa. Continuing Dr. Okpara said that he wanted to begin a sugar industry in eastern Nigeria; and he wanted Jamaican workers to assist. He said that he would be visiting Jamaica and would be in touch with us.

We had several visits from Mr. Adeoye who was insisting that we return to Jamaica; and even hinted that we might be arrested if we did not accept his terms.

I rejected his propositions and replied that we were not strangers to adversity; and we were prepared to go to jail in Nigeria, if that was what it took to accomplish our goals.

Eventually one evening in August, Mr. Adeoye visited us at Apapa Road and informed us that the government had decided to sponsor our mission to Kenya. They presented us with airline tickets to Nairobi, Kenya.

KENYA

Our mission arrived in Nairobi, the capital city of

Kenya; and we checked into the New Stanley Hotel. We immediately noticed a change in the climatic conditions. While Nigeria was mostly hot and humid, Nairobi's air was cool and brisk. While the city of Lagos was over crowded, Nairobi was verdant and more spacious. I took an immediate liking to Kenya.

After two days in the New Stanley Hotel we were visited by a Kenyan delegation, led by Mr. Paul Nduritu, who informed us that president "Miziwi" Jomo Kenyatta instructed them to offer us accommodations. We accepted his offer. Subsequently we were escorted by motorcade to a village on the slopes of Mount Kenya, about twenty six miles from Nairobi. The village was named Tinghanga in the Kiambu district. In the distance we could see Gitunguri, the home district of Jomo the "Burning Spear." We soon learned that we were in the midst of "Mau Mau Country". The Mau Maus were the freedom fighters who fought for the independence of Kenya.

Arriving in Tinghanga we were greeted by the entire tribal village of Kikuyu. The festivities lasted all evening until the wee hours of the morning. Brother Paul Nduritu was the chieftain of the village and a former captain in the Mau Mau revolutionary forces, which wrested Kenya's independence from Great Britain.

Brother Paul and others related many tales of Mau Mau activities in the Kiambu and Gitunguri areas during their struggle for independence. They reported many galant deeds, particularly some of the strategies of the notorious Mau Mau leader "General China". This general waged relentless attacks upon the British occupying forces.

Brother Paul was our elected liaison to the government. Our delegation met with Mr. Oginga Odinga,

Minister of the Interior. He was also a former Mau Mau freedom fighter. We stated the purpose of our mission and also asked that the government sponsor our trip to Ethiopia after our visit in Kenya. Mr. Odinga assured us that he would convey our request to President Kenyatta. We then visited the headquarters of the Kenyan African Nationalist Union (K.A.N.U.).

Here we met and conferred with Mr. Tom M'Boya, the Secretary General of K.A.N.U.

Just a few weeks after our meeting with Mr. M'Boya, he was assassinated by an unknown assailant. We also met with members of the Kenyan African Church, whose philosophy was based upon the divinity of His Imperial Majesty Emperor Haile Sellassie I. The brothers of the church all lived by the Nazarite vow-not shaving their hair. We were delighted to meet with these brethren half way around the world from Jamaica, with similar concepts as the Rastafarians in Jamaica.

All the tribes of Africa spoke their own tribal languages. However, in East Africa for instance Kenya, Uganda, Tanganyika, Zanzibar, and the areas of the Kenyan/Ethiopian border, the tribes spoke Swahili in addition to their tribal tongue. "Jambo Sana" and "Misouri San Sana" were greetings that bode you well as you travel in these areas.

In the Tinghanga/Kiambu area we received many request from various schools to lecture on the West Indies, particularly Jamaica. We complied with every request. The students were impeccably mannered and very attentive. They were enthused, and asked many questions. They were inspired by our lectures; many meeting people from the West Indies for the first time. The villagers embraced us with such hospitality that we felt like one big happy family among the Kikuyus. We were at home in every sense of the word.

During the evenings after dinner, the entire village assembled at Paul's home where they entertained us with folk songs, music, and cultural dance. Their musical instruments were mostly bamboo fifes, banjos, and drums. We responded by singing our own Rastafarian chants and beating the Akete drums, much to their delight. They unfolded their folklore, taught us some of the Kikuyu and Swahili language, and taught us some of their songs. We sang along with our Kikuyu family and felt the spirit of Mau Mau patriotism stirring inside our souls.

The Kiambu area had an abundance of coffee and citrus trees. The Kikuyus kept large herds of cows to provide them with milk and beef. We were well fed with fresh cow's milk, roast beef, corn (bembe), yams, plantains, okras, and peas and beans of all variety. The flavor of their coffee was exquisite.

On these slopes of Kenya, about two to three thousand feet high above sea level, the night air was very cool; and mornings filled the ground with heavy dew. The air remained cool and brisk, free from pollution. The people were of strong physique and appeared to be very healthy. At times, we were escorted from one village to another; usually a mountainous stroll of a few miles. Our feet were the mode of transportation. The environment was conducive to fitness.

We stayed about four months in Kenya. Then one day Brother Paul told us that a meeting was scheduled for us to meet with the minister of the interior. Escorted by Brother Paul, we journeyed down the mountains from Tinghanga to Nairobi. We met with Mr. Oginga Odinga who informed us that President Kenyatta wanted us to see the people's culture first hand, and that was his rea-

son for sending us to Kiambu district. Continuing Mr.
Odinga said that the government was ready to send us on
to Ethiopia.

That night, the villagers held a farewell party for us.
They prayed for us, expressed their love for us, and gave
us an open invitation to return. There was a mutual sad-
ness between us, although paradoxically we were happy
to continue our mission to Ethiopia. The next day we
departed on Ethiopian Airlines for Ethiopia.

Letter to the Kenya African Independent Communion Churches of East Africa

To whom it may concern:

The Council of Bishops of the Kenya African
Independent Communion churches of E.A. have met with
the delegates of the Jamaica Rastafari Back to Africa
Delegation which included Brothers Messrs Philmore
Alvaranga, Samuel Clayton and Douglas Mack and dis-
cussed the following items of importance.

1. The people of Kenya who have after a long struggle for independence against the imperialist, only recently gained it, very well recognize the struggle of their
brothers and the people of (the) African origin in Jamaica
an America etc. We recommend your stand and give you
this note as a sort of report to take back to our brother's
abroad carrying more facts on our difficulties to emanci-
pate our people.

2. This Council of Bishops of the Indigenous
Churches of Kenya working with the K.A.N.U. and its
parliamentarian and the government leaders strongly

support the return to Africa of the grandsons of Africa from Jamaica and the U.S.A. and else where in the world since their being in these foreign lands was not a mistake of their own but wicked work of the imperialists who had disturbed Africa in the past and now.

3. This moment being the 8th month since Kenya had its political independence delegation from Jamaica and our Council have learned much of our own difficulties in helping them and we instead have decided a joint effort and plan to enable their plan and our desire to succeed.

1. The council will acquire free lands from the African reserve lands for the settlement of more than 10,000 African origins from Jamaica and U.S.A. if only they can organize themselves with enough money to maintain themselves in the African reserves. These lands will be offered to these African descendants by the members of the Indigenous Churches according to our customs.

2. The Council of Bishops of the Indigenous Churches also authorize the delegates to appeal to the friends of Africa and the African descendants to donate and contribute to the building of the Indigenous Churches and schools here which during the emergency of 1952-60 were destroyed by the imperialists because the Indigenous Church was the source of opposition to the foreign rule as the present leaders of our government were the leaders of the Indigenous Church.

We are raising 9,000 pounds locally and we appeal to the African origins and friends to contribute 9,000 pounds for a building for the national guests and a church in Nairobi.

The building will serve as home for all those of African origins who return back to Africa, before they are settled in the reserve. Any cooperation with the struggling Africans of America and Jamaica is needed and important.

We demand special representative from Jamaica and elsewhere to come and help us in planning and preparing homes for the rest.

We remain yours in the struggle on behalf of the council of Bishops of the Indigenous Church of Kenya East Africa.

Felix Ndirangu.

ETHIOPIA

We disembarked at Addis Ababa International Airport in November of 1964. Upon our arrival the mission was met by members of the Ethiopian Patriarchate and representatives of the government. We were told that His Grace, the Abuna and patriarch of the Ethiopian Orthodox Church requested our presence at the Partriachate that very day. Kes Ermias was our elected liaison. He escorted us to the Partriachate, where we met with His Grace Abuna Theophilus and other members of the Orthodox Clergy. Our delegation was welcomed and blessed by His Grace the Abuna.

His Grace recalled our first visit to the Partriachate in 1961 when the Abuna Basilios, the then patriarch, conferred with the Rastafarian brothers of the mission-

Jamaican Rastafarian Back to Africa Delegation in Addis Ababa 1965. At the Imperial Palace. Brother Douglas Mack (center) addressing H.I.M. Emperor Haile Sellassie I, with the Emperor's Grand children.

Brother Philmore, Brother Planno, and I (Douglas Mack). Since that time the Abuna Basilios had passed away; and His Grace Abuna Theophilus was installed as the new head of the church. Our delegation stated our present mission's purpose:

a) To meet with His Imperial Majesty Emperor Haile Sellassie I, to formally present our petition in continuation of the 1961 mission's representation to the government of Ethiopia, regarding the resettlement of the Rastafarian brethren in Ethiopia.

b) To obtain an official reply to convey back to our Rastafarian brethren in Jamaica.

c) For the Ethiopian government to accommodate us until our mission was fulfilled.

His Grace replied that he would inform His Imperial Majesty of our mission's request; and that the Partriachate would cover our accommodations while we waited on His Majesty's reply. Next we visited the Imperial Palace where His Imperial Majesty was granting audience to the ambassadors of foreign countries. We took our position in line. When the emperor saw us he said in English, "Are you the Rastafarian brethren?" We responded, "Yes your majesty." We then presented the emperor with a petition referring to the genocidal action of the Jamaican government against the brethren; and a wooden carved globe with Africa and a large V embossed. "That's Africa!" he said. We explained that the carving symbolized Africa's spreading influence over the world. His Majesty thanked us for the gift and said

Rastafarian Back to Africa Delegation on the second mission to Africa 1964, at the office of Ato Tafara Kidane work, the minister of the Imperial Palace seated at right. Seated beside His Excellency Ato Tafara is Brother Douglas Mack. Addis Ababa, Ethiopia, 1964.

that he would give us an answer in due time. We each shook hands with him and then departed.

We resided at a hotel in Addis Markato (meaning new market). We made many friends there. Soon we began speaking the Amharic language which we learned from our new found friends in Addis Ababa. We learned the basics for giving directions, ordering our meals, and so on. We quickly learned how to haggle with merchants in the Ethiopian language over the price of goods in the marketplace. We attended several Orthodox Church services, including Saint Georges Church where the emperor worshiped regularly.

We also made daily visits to the Partriachate where we reasoned with many priests who were always present. Through these conversations we learned of the daily court hearings held by His Imperial Majesty, at the old palace of the former Emperor Menelik II. One day while we awaited the emperor's entourage on the way to one of his court sessions, His Imperial Majesty summoned his chauffeur to stop the car as he spotted us among the crowd. A police captain came to us to convey His Majesty's request for us to attend the Imperial Court session that day. We were escorted by the police captain and ushered to our seats in the court. We were informed that His Imperial Majesty held these court hearings regularly. At these sessions, the citizens could make personal appeals about decisions handed down by other courts. Hiring an attorney or advocate was optional. After hearing all the evidence, His Majesty would confer with his court advisors then pass his judgment, which was binding on the appellants. All the briefings were conducted in an Ethiopian language, so we did not understand what each individual case was about; but we could tell to whom a favorable judgment was made by that individual's antics. We later learned that most of these cases were about land disputes.

The city of Addis Ababa maintained a den of lions which they kept open to the public. We made many visits there and spent many hours observing the animals and their attendants' behavior.

One evening after observing the lions being fed, an attendant approached us and beckoned with his hands. He kept saying to us, "Na, na" (which meant come, come). We understood the gesture and went with the attendant, who was an elderly man of small stature, slim and wiry. The old man went to the main outer gate of the circular steel bar enclosure, pushed the gate up, and stepped inside. Then he beckoned for us to enter. We did and he closed the gate behind us.

For reasons beyond comprehension I had no fear whatsoever and had full confidence in the attendant, whom we never really knew. All three of us boldly stepped in the lion's den. He then led us through a passage to a another steel gate. He pushed it up and entered; then beckoned us to enter as well; which we did without hesitation. Immediately, about four full grown lions made a growling noise and approached us. Then the old man, with nothing but a staff in his hand, stood in front of us while the animals lumbered up to us. He shouted their names "Togo!" "Desta!" Then he waived his staff, rubbed their noses with his hands, and calmed them down. He then told us to take some photographs, which we did. Then he told us to touch the lions. I even pulled some hair from Togo's mane. This I took back to Jamaica with me and showed to the brethren. We stayed about ten minutes in the den with the lions continually circling around; but not menacingly. Finally the attendant instructed us to face the animals and back off slowly, one

step at a time to the gate. The whole time he was in front
of us until we were out of the den. Once we were outside
the den we shook hands together and had a long laugh
about the exploit.

The significance of the venture in the den never really dawn on me until we were out. It was then that I felt
the awe with some pride of courage, the gesture we enacted. Visions of Daniel in the lions' den then came to mind.

We visited Dr. Talbot, a West Indian from British
Guyana, whom we met in 1961. He was now employed
by the government of Ethiopia and was residing in Addis
Ababa. Dr. Talbot had a farm in Ambo, about two hundred kilometers from Addis Ababa. He told us that a
Jamaican Rastafarian brother was the overseer of his
farm. He invited us to visit the brother and spend some
time on the farm. We accepted his offer and soon after,
caught a bus ride to Ambo. Ambo was a quaint rural
town with much farmland.

Brother Moses was the overseer of Dr. Talbot's farm.
He migrated from Jamaica to England, where he lived for
a while before settling in Ethiopia. He resided on the farm
with his Ethiopian wife and children. We spent a week
with them. We went horseback riding daily around the
farm and adjoining areas. Brother Moses gave us a rifle
and advised us to always carry it with us because of the
hyenas and other wild animals, which prowled around
the area. Though we never had any encounter with the
prowling animals, we could hear them clearly in the still
of the night. Sometimes at nights we fired into the air to
scare the wild animals away. We all learned how to shoot
a rifle during our stay. Brother Moses often lined-up bot-
tles and we took turns at target practice.

Ambo was well known for its mineral spring; and
there was a water bottling company there. The mineral

water was called Ambo Wuha. We thoroughly enjoyed our visit on the farm. The countryside was like a breath of fresh air. After a week we went back to Addis Ababa.

We later visited the British Embassy in Addis Ababa, where we had a meeting with the ambassador. We expressed the purpose of our mission, recalling that we had sent a petition in 1961 to Her Majesty Queen Elizabeth II, seeking reparations to assist in resettling the Rastafarian brethren in Ethiopia. We asked the ambassador to inform Queen Elizabeth II to act on our petition of 1961. The ambassador said that he would inform Her Majesty's government of our mission's request. We noticed that the British Embassy was guarded and tended by Sudanese soldiers in their resplendent uniforms.

We made friends with many of them and visited them in their quarters frequently. They resided on the grounds of the embassy with their families. They were all of Islamic faith; but spoke English very well, which allowed us to converse freely with them.

Our visits to the Imperial Palace became quite frequent. We were well known in the palace circle, especially to Ato Tafara Kidane Worq who was the minister of the palace. On December 25, Christmas day, 1964 we visited the Imperial Palace for a special occasion. On this day, the emperor met members of the diplomatic corp. Also present was a choir from the United States Embassy who sang Christmas carols for His Imperial Majesty. This was an annual event and we were happy to be there. We enjoyed the carols very much.

OFFICIAL AUDIENCE WITH
HIS IMPERIAL MAJESTY

Finally one day in April of 1965, after nearly six months in Ethiopia, our delegation was summoned to an official audience with His Imperial Majesty. This was the climax; the purpose of our trek from Jamaica's shore. Up the palace steps and into the great red carpeted halls we strolled. As we looked straight ahead there was His Majesty standing on a dais, with his grand children all around him. Also in attendance was Ato Tafara Kidane Worq and other members of His Majesty's cabinet, along with His Grace, the Abuna Theophilus, and members of The Ethiopian Orthodox Clergy.

We bowed as we came before the emperor; and began chanting psalm 9 "I will praise Thee O Lord with my whole heart...". When we were finished, His Imperial Majesty greeted us; and addressing us directly said, "You have now been in Ethiopia long enough to understand some of the problems that face Ethiopia. Ethiopia, unlike other African states, was never conquered or subjugated by European colonial powers; and so throughout the years have had to fend for itself, without outside help." He went on to say, "Ethiopia never had a godfather, so to speak, as other African countries, who have now gained independence from the colonial powers." "These colonial powers now render some assistance to the development of these countries," he said. He also said, "Ethiopia had many problems to attend to. However, it would welcome the Rastafarian brethren to reside here." In continuance he said, "Ethiopia is a large country of over four hundred thousands square miles and has plenty of land available for resettlement." His Majesty said that the Sheshamane land grant was one of the areas, granted for resettlement of people of African descent residing in the western hemisphere, who desired to return. He also said that Ethiopia needed the skills of our brothers in the west to assist in her development; and his government would continue talks with the government of Jamaica towards that end. His Majesty went on to say that our delegation, upon returning to Jamaica, must assist in organizing and uniting the brethren and enlighten them with the facts about Ethiopia. The Emperor said that he would arrange for our return to Jamaica.

On behalf of our delegation I thanked His Imperial Majesty for the hospitality and accommodations granted to us during our stay in Ethiopia. We also thanked him for granting us an official reply to relate to our Rastafarian brethren in Jamaica. Subsequently, on behalf of the Rastafarians I extended an invitation to His Majesty to visit Jamaica. At this point his Imperial Majesty gave each of us a gold coin to commemorate our visit. He then promised to visit Jamaica in the near future.

Our return passage was arranged for scheduled stops in London, New York, and Kingston, Jamaica. This was to enable us to communicate with our affiliated organizations prior to our return to Jamaica.

OUR RETURN JOURNEY HOME

In April 1965, our mission departed from Addis Ababa for London, England. Upon arrival, we were met by some brethren and were escorted to Frankie "Reds" McCook's home. He was the elder brother of Tommy McCook, of "Skatalite" fame. We stayed two weeks with Frankie and during this time we conferred with many brethren and acquaintances about our recent African mission. At the end of the two weeks we departed from

London for New York.

Upon arrival in New York, we immediately visited our organization the A.R.C. and the House of Judah. To our dismay, we found the A.R.C. was in disarray; with many brethren abstaining from weekly attendance. After investigating the circumstances we found that against our advice during our absence, Brother Robinson led a delegation of the A.R.C. to Jamaica, which included the general secretary and the treasurer. He was attempting to establish a branch of the A.R.C. in Jamaica. We found that he had been declared "persona non gratia" by the government of Jamaica, and was sent back to the United States.

Before our trip to Africa we had discussed the possibility of establishing a branch of the A.R.C. in Jamaica with members of the organization. However, we instructed Brother Robinson to wait until our arrival back from our African tour when we would have a reply from His Imperial Majesty. We would then lead our A.R.C. delegates to Jamaica and establish a branch there.

We distinctly warned Brother Robinson that the brethren in Jamaica would reject any incursion by him into the prerogatives of Rastafari, without our presence. We learned that Brother Robinson ignored our counsel and arbitrarily visited Jamaica. We also learned that his visit led to a lot of confusion among the brethren as to its purpose. Disturbances occurred during his meetings and much controversies developed as a result.

From reports we learned that Brother Planno quickly married Sister Sandiford, the treasurer of our African Repatriation Committee (A.R.C.). Subsequent action by Brother Robinson's group led to a police investigation and Brother Robinson's expulsion from the island.

Sister Sandiford was arrested upon arrival at New

York International Airport for illegal importation of marijuana. This was the first time that Sister Sandiford had
ever left the United States; and she was duped into this
misadventure.

Consequently, as soon as we arrived in New York
from our tour of Africa, the FBI summoned us to a meeting. The officer in charge stated that they had investigated our organization (the A.R.C.) after the arrest of our
treasurer. They subsequently received reports from the
Criminal Investigation Department (C.I.D.) in Jamaica
concerning the activities of the A.R.C. officers in Jamaica.
The FBI had suspicions that the A.R.C.'s purpose was to
establish an international drug ring. We refuted these
allegations; and told the FBI officers that we did not have
control over members individual activities. Furthermore
the alleged activities occurred during our absence and
was unknown to us. In addition, we told the investigating officers that the purpose of our organization was to
establish repatriation of our brethren to Africa.

At the end of the meeting, the FBI stated that their
government had no problems with our mission delegates,
or our mission's purpose in the United States, and that
there would be no prejudice against our future travels to
the United States.

We felt totally disgusted after we left the meeting
with the FBI, by the irrational activities of Brother
Robinson and with the persons who duped Sister
Sandiford. They had ripped apart, in an instance of self-
ishness, that which we spent so much time and effort to
build.

I recalled the trials and tribulations of the Honorable
Marcus Garvey; and how some of his own, helped to
undermine and ruin the foundations of the U.N.I.A. in
New York. Nevertheless, our mission fortified our

resolve to bridge all gaps and organize our brethren into a united body in Jamaica.

In May of 1965, we arrived back in Jamaica. At the airport in Kingston we were greeted with drumming and chanting by a multitude of brethren; and had an official police escort to the National Heroes Park, where we held a public meeting. The people reacted with overwhelming adulation, rejoicing in the accomplishment of our mission. This later led to the formation of the Rastafarian Brethren Repatriation Association (the R.B.R.A.). We assisted some of our members to resettle in Sheshamane, Ethiopia where they still reside.

Though we remitted a report to the government of Jamaica, requesting that they collaborate with the respective African governments in regards to our resettlement in Africa, the Jamaican government remained dormant to the purpose. The exodus of African sons and daughters from the western hemisphere to the motherland, has yet to materialize. Africa awaits!

"DECLARATION OF REPATRIATION AND REHABILITION" PETITION 1963

To Her Majesty Queen Elizabeth II of England, Commander in chief of the Commonwealth of Nations. Protector of the British Empire and to Her Majesty's government!!!

May it Please your Majesty:

We the people of African descent, domiciled in Jamaica, West Indies, through the era of Slave Trading, who have been granted lands for resettlement in the

Empire of Ethiopia. Through the generosity of His Imperial Majesty Emperor Haile Sellassie I, King of Kings, Ruler of Ethiopia; do here by now beseech Her Majesty and Government, through the Justice of Almighty God, and through the powers of this petition, to assist us with a ship for transportation, and equipment necessary for us to resettle and rehabilitate ourselves on the land!!! (graciously granted by H.I.M. Emperor Haile Sellassie I).

We the people of African descent domiciled in Jamaica, West Indies, who desires Repatriation to Ethiopia, do hereby ask Her Majesty Queen Elizabeth II of England and Her Majesty's Government to assist our Repatriation Requirements, submitted on this Petition!!!

This we ask of Her Majesty through our representatives Philmore Alvaranga, Samuel Clayton, Douglas Mack, Rastafarian Brethren Ambassadors, for the Back to Africa Movement.

Brief History Concerning Jamaica. On May 4th 1494, Christopher Columbus the Spanish navigator came upon the Island now known as Jamaica on his second voyage to the New World. Spanish rule started over the Island in 1509 when Juan de Esquivel came to govern the island as a colony of Spain. Christopher Columbus had met Arawak Indians who inhabited the Island, Juan de Esquivel made slaves of the Arawak Indians and in about 50 years of Spanish rule the Arawaks were exterminated. African Slaves were then brought to work on the Spanish plantations.

The Spanish ruled Jamaica for 146 years, until 1655.

BRITISH RULE

On May 10th 1655, British forces under Commander Admiral Penn and General Venables, sent out by Oliver Cromwell, landed in Jamaica and engaged the Spanish forces in battle, the African slaves who were called maroons, played an active part against the Spanish rulers, and the next day May 11, 1655, the Spanish surrendered and British rule over the Island commenced. Britain continued to bring African slaves by the thousands to Jamaica, and the island became known as a central slave market in the New World and resort of English Buccaneers and pirates. The most notorious buccaneer was Henry Morgan who later became governor of Jamaica. The most notorious slave trader who brought African slaves to Jamaica was John Hawkins, and in 1564, Queen Elizabeth I gave John Hawkins her personal ship S.S. Jesus of Lubeck and a Royal Charter to transport slaves from Africa to the West Indies!

The Spanish and the British rulers, always told the slaves to work until Jesus come, but in 1567 the S.S. Jesus was sunk. The Hard oppression upon the Africans caused them to rebel repeatedly against the British, there was major rebellions in 1663, 1690.

In 1694 the French fleet under Admiral Ducasse attacked Jamaica, again the African slaves fought gallantly against the French invaders, helping the British to drive them back to their ships, but the French succeeded in destroying 50 sugar estates and captured nearly 2000 slaves, before bring driven off the Island.

In 1704 the African slaves again rebelled for freedom and during this year some estates owned by the British were burned down.

In 1728 General Cudjoe an African slave led a major

rebellion for freedom. This Maroon slave rebellion was so strong the British had to bring two regiments of soldiers from Gibraltar, and imported hundreds of blood hound dogs. The British attacked Nanny Town a maroon settlement. The battle was one of the fiercest ever fought in Jamaica. Thousands of slaves were killed, and the British burnt down the town, but the Maroons rallied soon after that battle and surrounded a British force of sailors and soldiers massacreing them.

1738 Edward Trelawny the British governor sent to Nicaragua, South America, for Mosquito Indians, to help fight the Africans, but the African slaves fought for freedom so fiercely that, governor Trelawny signed a peace treaty with the Maroons. 1746 another uprising by the Africans against their slavery. 1760 another uprising by the slaves who captured Port Maria a town, the battle was bloody the British killed over 500, and deported over 1000 to British Honduras. In 1762 Henry Lyttleton the governor, asked the slaves to join an expedition against the Spanish in Cuba, the African slaves helped the British to capture Havana, but the British gave it back when a peace treaty was signed!!! The slaves continued to rebel time after time for freedom, which never came. There were rebellions in 1808-1809, 1818-1829, 1831, 1833-1853. On the 28th August the British Parliament passed a law whereby from 1834-1840 every slave in the British Empire should be set free. 20,000 million pounds (British currency) was provided as compensation to the slave owners, but none provided for the slaves who underwent the torture and pain. August 1st, 1838, Queen Victoria of England proclaimed emancipation for all slaves. This was indeed a noble act, but the slaves still received no compensation for our years of torture and suffering.

Appeal to Her Majesty Queen Elizabeth II, your

Majesty, we must focus your attention to the fact that, Sierra-Leone, and also Liberia, was founded for the purpose of resettling African slaves, both Freetown and Liberia was aided by the British and American governments, and we state the above historical facts not as a base for grievance against the British crown, but as an appeal for assistance to resettle in Africa, which the above historical facts will show that we are deserving of assistance from the British government.

MISSION TO AFRICA

In 1961, the government of Jamaica sponsored a mission to five African countries to seek the resettlement of people of African descent in Ethiopia, Nigeria, Ghana, Liberia and Sierra-Leone, and in conjunction with this mission of which we were elected delegates, the British government, agreed to help in such a resettlement scheme, we now take this opportunity to remind Her Majesty and Her Majesty's government of such a promise, yet to be fulfilled. At present we have been granted lands in Ethiopia through the Humane instrumentality of His Imperial Majesty Emperor Haile Sellassie I, Might Conquering Lion of Judah, and it is in the boldness of justice that we ask the British government, for assistance in the form of a ship and mechanical equipment, to develop the land.

Commonwealth Migration Ban. Britain has now closed her doors to commonwealth migration and this has also affected Jamaica adversely, Jamaica is only 4500 square miles with a population of nearly (2,000,000) two million people. One third of the land is not arable and industry is only just developing, hence, Jamaica has a chronic unemployment problem, and is dangerously overpopulated. The closing of the British doors have now worsened these two problems. Every effort should now be made by the British government, to encourage the Back to Africa movements, and to assist the people of African descent who lives in the west, and desires to return home, (for Africa is the original home of all African peoples). The British government should also urge Jamaica's government, by advising the government to face the problems of the Back-to-Africa Movements squarely and sincerely.

BRITAIN'S POLICY IN WORLD AFFAIRS

Your Majesty, we must say that judging from history Britain's past role in world affair, has always been appreciated by the peoples of underdeveloped countries, the reward of Britain's policy in the world, is the high esteem in which Britain is held internationally and especially here in Africa.

History shows that Britain was perhaps the last European nation to deal in the African slave trade. Portugal, Spain and France, preceeded Britain in slave trading. And it was Britain who first did something about stopping the practice, through the persons of William Wilberforce and HM Queen Victoria, who proclaimed emancipation for the slaves throughout the British Empire. In the past, Britain was not afraid to let other slave trading nations like Spain and France, know that Britain would oppose the practice by whatsoever means at her disposal. Those policies of Britain was indeed gallant.

Today at present, Britain,'s high esteem in Africa has increased instead of decreasing, not only by our humble opinion, but by judging from the recent political emancipation especially in Africa, for this political emancipation your majesty is to be personally congratulated as a Heroine of Justice, spiritually and physically; and we must also add that the wind of change witnessed in Africa today, will become the greatest asset to the British nation in the years to come since Africa as a whole is the richest continent in natural resources.

Your majesty it is imperative to Britain's honor and future, the existing conditions of Southern Rhodesia and South Africa. We will not go into the history of Britain in regards to those two particular parts of Africa, suffice it to say that Britain must see, that spiritual and political justice be given to the Africans living in Southern Rhodesia, and South Africa, and Britain must remain unflinching and unfailing to her duty to justice. Ethiopia will always remember the Justice of Britain, by the aid Ethiopia received during the her hour of greatest need, when the very existence and survival of the Ethiopian nation was at stake. Generals Cunningham and Wingate, are names never to be forgotten in Ethiopian history. Your majesty by granting to the petitioners, the necessary aid of transportation and equipment, to enable us to develop our community on the lands made available to us in Ethiopia, we are sure that in the process of time Britain will be rewarded by us for such works, and the future relations of Britain and Ethiopia will be made secure, (as it is written unto all mankind, "Thou shalt Love thy neighbour as thyself. We the signees of this petition, sincerely hope, that Your majesty and Her Majesty's government, take this petition in earnest sincerity and, give your approval to materialize this plea.

Chapter 11

H.I.M. EMPEROR HAILE SELLASSIE VISITS JAMAICA

"Behold the lion of the tribe of Judah!"

The morning was bleak, with drizzling rain on Thursday, April 21, 1966. The clouds obscured the usual bright tropic morning sunshine. All the Rastafarian brethren island-wide arose early, making final preparations. On our camp at Glasspole Avenue in Warieka Hills, we had early morning chanting and "ishence" burning as we assembled the brethren in order to proceed to Palisadoes and Norman Manley Airport.

With Count Ossie and the African Drum Reverberations, and the brethren dressed in splendid red, gold and green regalia, Brothers Phil, Sam and I groomed in our Ethiopian national robes, led a throng of brethren in a motorcade down from the hills. The motorcade was preceded by a motor cycle squad, captained by Brother Fairweather. We were cheered on by the crowd gathered by the roadside as we turned on Windward Road, heading for the airport. This was a momentous day in the Historic Annals of Jamaica. The day of the arrival of the "Lion of Judah," Emperor Haile Sellassie I.

When we arrived at the airport, the police directed us to our designated area. I protested to the officer. At the very lease, Brother Phil and I expected to be on the tarmac with the official protocol welcome group. After all, it was Brothers Phil, Planno and I who extended the invitation to His Imperial Majesty to visit Jamaica during our mission to Ethiopia in April, 1961. Now that the Emperor's visit was imminent, we were officially snubbed by our own Government. Nothing however, could dim the aura and spirit of this occasion.

There were a multitude of brethren and supporters gathered at the airport. Over 100,000 was the conservative figures. They came to get a glimpse of the legendary Ethiopian Potentate. Brethren from everywhere, mixed in a sea of red, green and gold were greeting each other. The police for the first time displayed a friendly accommodation towards us. Many groups of brethren including Count Ossie and our Warieka Hills crew, were beating the akete drums, chanting and dancing as we anxiously awaited the moment of his Majesty's arrival.

The rain was still drizzling, then suddenly, the clouds briefly dissipated and the bright tropical sun burst through and almost immediately, the multitude sent up a roar as a plane appeared in the distant . All eyes went shooting towards the sky, in an instant another roar went out from the throng, as the distinct marking of the Ethiopian colors became visible. There was no denying, this was "Jah" riding on the wings of the wind.

The air was filled with tumultuous roar from the multitude and shouts of "Jah Rastafari."

On the tarmac, the government officials waited at the plane's step to greet the Emperor. A quiet stillness overcame the crowd as we waited impatiently in anticipation for a few minutes. The plane's door suddenly opened, there he stood, dressed in his military Field Marshall uniform. "Behold the Conquering Lion of the Tribe of Judah, the Root and the Offspring of David."

Brother Roy, from the hills, over come with emotion at the sight of the legendary Monarch, sped from the

crowd towards the plane. His dashed triggered a sponta-
neous reaction from the crowd which overwhelmed the
authorities present. The plane was mobbed.

In the confusion that prevailed, His Imperial Majesty
could not alight from the aircraft. Realizing what was
happening, I tried to get to the plane, but the crowd was
in a fr enzy and it became impossible for me to get
through. I espied Brother Planno breaking through and
he ascended the steps to the plane. He stood there and
shouted to the throng, "Step back and allow His Majesty
to alight." The crowd retreated a few steps backward and
Brother Planno led His Imperial Majesty down the steps
with his Chihuahua dog. The government officials were
so relieved, they whisked the Emperor to the awaiting
limousine. The streets of Kingston were live with people
cheering wildly as the motorcade drove through to King's
House, the home of Jamaica's first native Governor
General, Sir Clifford Campbell.

The Emperor's visit lasted for three days. Jamaicans
were always relentlessly enthused to see and greet him.
The itinerant set for His Majesty's visit were:

A ceremony in honor of him at the national stadium.
The stadium was jam packed when he arrived. The
crowd swelled from his procession of followers. He met
with the Joint House of Parliament at Gordon House. He
visited Jamaica House, the residence of the Prime
Minister, Sir Alexander and Lady Bustamante.

During his rounds, he toured the different colleges in
Kingston. The College of Arts, Science and Technology,
Mico Teacher's Training Center, The University of the
West Indies. At the university, he addr essed a special
convocation and was conferred with a Honorary Doctor
of Law degree. The visit to Payne Avenue site was most
memorable. He laid the first block for the Haile Sellassie

I school, which he donated to the Jamaican people.

Brother Phil, Sam and I were guest of His Majesty at the luncheon at Vale Royal with acting Prime Minister, Donald Sangster. It was a feast to remember. We presented a pair of reading lamps crafted from Jamaica's mahoe tree as a token of our appreciation to His Majesty. During our conversation in the presence of the acting Prime Minster, His Majesty asked me which ministry of government I worked for. The acting Prime Minster was agape. I replied, "none your majesty, I am at the moment unemployed." He was shocked at my reply. He asked his aide to make a note of what was said.

Many Rastafarian brethren were invited to the ball in his honor at the Sheraton New Kingston Hotel. People were curious to know if the brethren questioned His Majesty regarding their claim that he is the returned Messiah, of whom the scriptures spoke.

I remember saying confidently without fear of successful contradiction that, Act of the Apostles, Chapter 2, verse 28-29, states, "From the fruit of David's loins, according to the flesh, God shall rise up Christ to sit upon David's throne. There was no doubt that Emperor Haile Sellasie I was the only living family by flesh and blood lineage sitting upon David's throne." That's gospel, Selah.

On April 23, His Majesty toured the rural areas of Jamaica using our steam engine train. He was graciously received at May Pen, Williamsfield, Manchester, Magotty, St. Elizabeth and Montego Bay. He gave his final salutation at the Montego Bay International Airport on April 24. The Lion ascended the Ethiopian aircraft we all watched in awe.

The Emperor Haile Sellasie visit left a lasting impression. Impeccable mannerism displayed by the Emperor throughout his tour of Jamaica. This historical visit can never be rivaled by any other visitor to Jamaica.

ABOUT THE AUTHOR

Douglas Mack was born and raised in the Eastern section of Kingston Jamaica, known as Rockfort Gardens. This area is on the plains under the slopes and shadows of the majestic Warieka Hills. Growing up, he became acquainted with all the Rastafarian brethren in the area and developed an intimate knowledge of the Rastafarian philosophical and religious culture.

Eventually, he became an ar dent advocate of the Rastafarian "Back-to-Africa" movement and was selected by the brethren to represent them on two successive missions to many coutnries in Africa, Europe, United States and the United Nations.

He is a founder and an ambassador of the African Repatriation Committee (ARC) in New York. He was also the founder and administrator for the Rastafarian Brethren Repatriation Association (R.B.R.A.) in Rennocklodge East Kingston, Jamaica.

During 1965, he was involved in several theater productions. His best known work was as Deacon Paul Bogle in "A Ballad for Rebellion 1865," a Sylvia Wynters narrative of the Morant Bay uprising of 1865.

His profound knowledge of the Rastafarian philosophy, ardent advocacy and administrative expertise of the culture and the constant urging of his family and brethren have inspired this literary work. Hopefully this book will leave a lasting and pellucid impression for posterity on its readers.